A   fe

Seacoas
Birmingham, Alabama

Cover illustration by Carol Middleton
*Chief Tuskaloosa shows Alabama to Spanish explorer
Hernando De Soto*

Published by Seacoast Publishing, Inc.
110 12th Street North
Birmingham, Alabama 35203

Illustrator: Steve Parker

Cover illustration copyright © Carol Middleton

ISBN 1-878561-25-1

To obtain copies of this book, please write or call:
Seacoast Publishing, Inc.
110 12th St. North
Birmingham, AL 35203
(205) 250-8016

I dedicate this book to my family--Anne Crump Nall, Carole A. Bennighof and Clarke J. Stallworth III. They always liked my stories.

Table of Contents

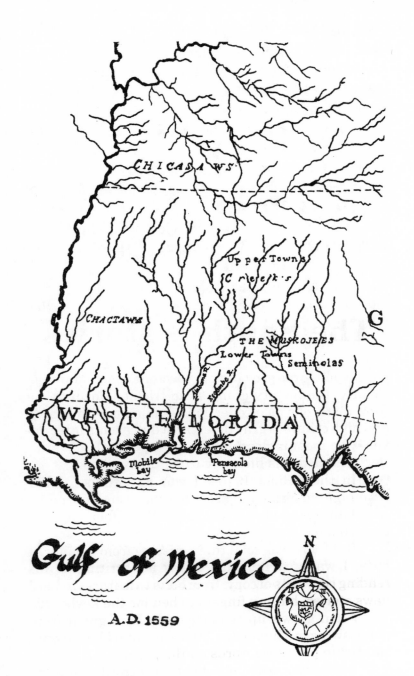

Preface

The South is stories

When I was growing up a doctor's son in Marengo County, the history of my state trickled down to me from textbooks as a collection of old men with beards and high collars, a gray tapestry of dull events interwoven with meaningless dates.

I carried this lifeless vision into manhood.

In the middle 1970s, I was city editor of *The Birmingham News*, a reasonably successful journalist who had abandoned writing for the higher pay and questionable prestige of an editor's job.

But there was something missing from my life. At base, I was a writer, and I was not writing. I was reading copy, lots of copy, from obits to features to hard news stories, but my fingers itched for the keyboard.

I had grown up reading books in a green front porch swing in Thomaston, Alabama, and I had always wanted to put those words on the page.

But now, with my brain eternally playing

catch-up with too much copy and not enough help on the desk, what would I write? I looked around for some subject which hadn't been spoken for. I couldn't just go out and poach on somebody else's beat.

So I created my own beat, a new one. An idea bubbled to the top of my mind: How about the stories out of Alabama history? Nobody had staked out that claim, and Alabama history could not possibly be as dull as the history textbooks made out.

The idea crystallized into a plan. I would find the facts and write them, in narrative style, as stories, and maybe I could make them interesting to newspaper readers.

I took an afternoon off from the obits and the telephone calls of the city desk, and went over to the Birmingham Public Library. Mary Bess Kirksey and her friends in the Southern History Room thought I had a good idea.

They pitched in to help: Mary Bess, Tom Miller, Yvonne Crumpler, Ann Tyler and later, Jennie Kimbrough Scott and Anne Knight.

They dug out books, marked the interesting places, and had them piled on the table when I got to the fourth floor. They looked up facts for me, they remembered their own favorite stories out of Alabama's past. They thought history was alive, and fun.

So I bent over the books in the library, burrowed beneath the surface of Alabama history, and found a treasure — jeweled stories glittering in the fluorescent library light.

There, just beneath the gray surface, were the people. Fighting, living, loving, rescuing each other, robbing each other, killing each other. Heroes, heroines, outlaws, saints, greedy people, pitiful people, mean people, weak people and people with wills like iron rods.

And their stories. Oh, their stories. The truth, better than the novels I had read in that front porch swing on that Thomaston front porch. Great things, shameful things, fascinating things, human things, ranging up and down the warp and woof of Alabama history like a golden thread.

So, in *The Birmingham News* on Sundays, I began to write stories out of Alabama history. I called it "A Day in the Life of Alabama." Some were all right, some were downright dull, and some of them were pretty good. I look at some of them now, and get that writer's tingle: Hey, I wrote that.

I took some license with the stories. I bridged some gaps with my imagination, based on the facts available. I did my homework, and the stories are historically accurate.

Ray Brown and Benny Yates of *The News* illustrated the stories, and their pictures made the stories come alive.

People read them. Teachers clipped them, and used them to help teach Alabama history to children. Maybe they helped some kid to know that Alabama history was alive, not dead.

Now and then, somebody would stop me on my way up 20th Street to the YMCA at lunch time, and tell me he liked the story last Sunday about the Confederate spy, or the pioneer woman. I liked that.

The message began to filter back to me: Other people were fed up with the idea of Alabama history as a collection of colorless, bloodless, cardboard figures. They were hungry for stories too.

The stories seemed to give people a better handle on their place. To know who did what, 200 years ago or 25 years ago, seemed to help them understand themselves better.

To me, it was more than that. It was like pulling a gauzy veil, a curtain, back from a stage. Once I had seen dull gray figures standing stiffly, motionless, on that stage of history.

Now, with the curtain pulled back, I saw living,

breathing, fighting, bleeding, loving, hating, working, people. To me, each story I wrote added another character to my stage.

I remember going on a midshipman cruise on a destroyer out of Newport, Rhode Island, in the late 1940s, when I was in the Naval ROTC program at Chapel Hill. On the destroyer were students from the great Ivy League universities.

Alabama was something to be ashamed of — first in poverty, last in education; first in hookworm and pellagra, last in literacy; first in hickdom and redneckery, last in culture. And if we escaped the bottom rung in any category, thank God for Mississippi.

And besides, we had lost the war. Glorious in defeat, certainly, shades of knights of old in a Walter Scott novel, and the keening, indomitable sound of a Rebel yell coming from that ragged gray line, moving across the meadow. But we had lost.

That was one thing the old Alabama history textbooks did well. They made defeat seem like victory, somehow.

At North Carolina, I had dreams of playing Edward R. Murrow, talking with a deep authoritative voice into New York microphones. I talked endlessly into a recorder, sitting in the attic of the SAE house, trying to strip away the levels of my Southern accent. I learned to say "North CArolina" instead of "Nawth CahLIna."

And that, to me now, is somehow sad.

All the Southern stereotypes on radio and television were fools, thick accents dripping with ignorance. I didn't want to be a Senator Claghorn, suh, so I learned to say "North CArolina."

Since then, I have come full circle. With the rich images of my Alabama stories in my head, I have become a Southern — and an Alabama — chauvinist.

We are not only as good as people from other regions of America, we are better off. And it is not football that makes it so.

We Southerners are distinctive. Our stories, our land, our heritage, makes us different. Southerners, and especially Alabamians, are lucky. We are simply more interesting than people who live in other places. Our stories make it so.

Don't misunderstand me. I know we have large problems in Alabama and the South. I know we are defensive, prickly, too quick to raise our fists. I know our schools are not high quality.

We need more high tech skills, we need more intelligent diversification of our industries, we need a better-educated workforce. We need to splice higher education and research together, our ticket into the future. We need tax reform, so that the timber and pulp companies pay their fair share of property tax, and channel more tax money into our starving schools.

We have many needs, no doubt about that. We are always playing catch up with the rest of the nation. But there is a bright side, even to that dark coin.

In the South, we are late bloomers. We were held back, and the calculated economic punishment after the Civil War has turned into a blessing.

If we were held back, by discriminatory freight rates or the sneers of Eastern money, our luck was holding.

So far, we have escaped the layers of sterile grayness they call progress in some places. We have not, as yet, sold our birthright for a mess of technological porridge. I hear they have a great porridge restaurant in Atlanta, just off Peachtree.

By starting late, we still have a chance to make technology serve us, do what we want it to do. We have a chance to join enlightened technology with our rich heritage, and create a humane life worth living.

The way we can come to maturity as a state, as a

people, is to know ourselves — where we are, what we are, who we are. If we position ourselves between our past and our future, we can walk forward with knowledge and confidence and pride. And we can be happy doing it.

But we can only position ourselves — find out who and where and what we are — by knowing our past, by knowing our stories. We don't have to agree with all the things in our heritage, but we must know about them, and accept them.

To me, stories are magic. They helped me to find myself as a writer, to know where I am and who I am. And there is a lot of joy, both in listening to stories and in telling them.

My friend, come closer to the fire, let me tell you about some people, in a place called Alabama.

The
Stories

Chapter One

11,000 B.C.

Alabama caveman: How did he die?

The man stood at the edge of the clearing, behind the thick clump of bushes, and watched the small deer nibble at a tuft of grass in the clearing.

Never taking his eyes off the deer, the man freed his right arm from his fur cloak. He fitted a short spear onto his atlatl, the spear-throwing stick. Then, suddenly, he moved quickly through the brush and raised his atlatl to throw.

The deer, startled at the sound in the brush, looked up once and leaped into the trees at the edge of the woods.

The man's arm came down, the atlatl launched

the spear, but it rattled harmlessly off a tree as the deer's white tail disappeared among the trees.

The man uttered a snort of disgust, an angry grunt, and walked across the clearing to pick up his spear.

Halfway across the clearing, he stopped. His nostrils twitched, and he turned his head, sniffing the air. He caught the scent of another human, a musky smell, close by.

The man crouched, then he broke into a run for the edge of the clearing. Just before he reached the treeline, a spear arched through the air, and the stone tip sliced into his back. A sharp cry of pain, and he fell, tumbling, into the bushes. He jumped up, looked behind once with wide eyes of fear, and limped quickly into the woods.

He threw himself into a creek bed, and splashed down the shallow stream, trying to get home. He heard the shrill cries of his enemies, crashing in the brush behind him, but the stream covered his trail.

He climbed out of the creek, whimpering softly. He reached behind him, but he couldn't reach the spear. He dragged himself up onto the lip of a huge cave, and then he fell. Women, who had been gathering nuts and seeds from the woods, carrying them in bags of skins, came running. Their sharp cries of distress echoed through the woods.

The women pulled the wounded man into the cave and tried to make him comfortable. They pulled the wooden stick from his back, and he writhed in pain. The spear point remained, a lump under the skin.

Finally, late in the afternoon, his cries stopped, and he died.

Toward nightfall, the men began to appear, coming through the trees, carrying wild turkeys, some squirrels and two came dragging a small bear they had killed.

More sounds of distress, sharp grunts of anger, as

they saw their dead brother. Some of them made warlike noises, growling, they would kill the enemies who had done this.

As the dead man lay in a corner of the cave, the women went about cooking supper. They lit their bear bone lamps — bones hollowed out and filled with bear grease — and began to cook the meat. They put hot stones into a skin bag with the squirrels, and the steaming hot water cooked the meat.

Later on that night, after the members of the group had finished their meal, several of the men hollowed out a hole in the earth floor of the cave and buried the man — with the spear point still in his back.

Thousands of years later, Carl F. Miller, leader of the Smithsonian Institution/National Geographic Society Russell Cave Expedition, was helping to dig in the cave.

His wife, Ruth Miller, came upon the skeleton of the man who had been killed with a spear, on that day almost 13,000 years ago.

As they scraped the earth away from his skeleton, Mrs. Miller paused. She saw the spear point lodged near the man's backbone.

"Carl," she said, "This man was killed."

Archeologists, digging in what is now called Russell Cave, have been able to recreate the kind of lives Alabamians lived thousands of years before Christ.

Generally, they found that cavemen of early Alabama times used Russell Cave for a shelter for thousands of years.

As the trash built up on the floor of the cave — bones, remains of fires, even bodies — the cavemen brought piles of dirt and covered the garbage, and leveled out a clean, flat floor.

The levels of the floor are a sort of time clock, layers of history which waited to be peeled back.

The Stone Age Alabamian lived and died in the time when David slew Goliath and later brought Israel to greatness.

On a dawning of that faraway time, the rising sun poured light into the mouth of the cavern, 107 feet wide and 27 feet high.

Just below the opening flowed Dry Creek, which pours into a large cave next door. Russell Cave is connected to the water-fed cavern, and is cooled by the air from the big cave, a sort of prehistoric air conditioning unit.

This probably explains why the cave was so attractive to early Alabama cave people — it offered shelter, protection from wild animals and human enemies, and in the summer, they even had cool air.

On a typical morning long ago, the men moved out of the cave and into the woods, carrying their stone axes and spears. They hunted deer, bear, turkey, raccoon, rabbit, turtle and snake. If hunting was poor, they scoured the woods for berries and nuts.

While the men hunted, the women and older girls squatted in the opening of the cave, working. Some of them scraped bear hides with stone knives, or sewed leather bags from deerskins.

Naked children played, running and shouting, in the space between the cave mouth and the creek.

There were no bows and arrows here, and few tools. The men used the atlatl (an Aztec name for the spear-throwing stick) and stone axes. The women used stone knives to scrape skins and cut meat. Tips of deer antlers were used to chip spear points and ax heads from flinty stone.

The women — and probably men too — used bone pins to tuck their hair at the back of their necks, keeping it out of their faces.

Shortly after 1,000 B.C. — almost 3,000 years ago — the Indians began moving out of Russell Cave. Sometimes hunters stayed there overnight — unaware of the layers of history beneath their feet — but the basic way of life had changed.

Now the wandering Indians — who had used Russell Cave as a way station — began to settle down. They stopped following the game, and began to live in houses, in permanent villages.

They learned to put seeds in the ground, and wait for the harvest. And they began to farm the rich bottomlands near the rivers.

Chapter Two

1540 A. D.

DeSoto vs. Tuskaloosa: The mystery of Maubila

By the time Columbus almost discovered America in 1492 (He never saw the mainland of North America.), the crude Indian villages had grown into cosmopolitan cities and complicated civilizations.

Streets were laid out, public buildings were raised, elaborate governments and religions were set up. There were the rich civilizations of the Aztecs in Mexico, the

Mayans in Central America, the Incas in Peru. Following close behind Columbus were the conquistadors, Spanish soldiers of fortune, with their horses and their armor and their insatiable lust for gold.

They slaughtered Indians by the thousands and enslaved the rest. And the Spanish galleons rode low in the water, going back to Cadiz, from the weight of the stolen gold.

In 1520, Hernando Cortez overthrew the great Aztec king, Montezuma, and laid his iron fist on Mexico.

One of the Indian tribes which lived under Montezuma, before the Spanish came, was the Muscogee. After Cortes took over, the Muscogees packed up their belongings — what they could carry on foot — and left their ancestral lands in the northwest part of Mexico.

They crossed the Rio Grande and headed up into what is now the United States. They forded the Red River, ranging all the way north to the Missouri River. Then a turn to the east to the Ohio River, and a right turn to the south, following the warm weather along the Mississippi River.

Finally, they headed eastward into what is now Alabama and Georgia.

In 1519, a Spanish commander named Alonzo de Pineda sailed into Mobile Bay with four ships. He named it Bahia Espiritu Santo, the Bay of the Holy Ghost.

In 1528, Panfilo de Narvaez landed at Tampa Bay and set out overland to the north and west, looking for gold along the sandy Florida beaches. He missed connections with his fleet, and he and his men were soon starving. They killed their horses and ate them, using the horsehides to make flimsy, low-in-the-water leather boats.

From the Florida Panhandle, he turned his rickety boats toward Mexico, which he thought was just down the coast. They landed near Mobile, then moved on down the coast to the west. Narvaez's boats were swept out to sea in a storm near the mouth of the Mississippi.

In May of 1539, Hernando De Soto landed in Tampa Bay with four ships, 600 men, 123 horses and several pigs. The pigs were driven along with the expedition; De Soto wanted to make sure his men had meat.

De Soto ranged to the north and west, discovered Pensacola Bay, and moved onto the north and east. Up through Georgia, all the way east to the Savannah River, then north to the Blue Ridge Mountains of the Carolinas.

Then De Soto turned west and south, going down the valley of the Tennessee River, down into Alabama. He was looking for gold. He found disaster.

* * * * * * * * * * * * *

A strange quiet lay over the Indian town.

The steel armor of the Spanish soldiers clanked as they walked through the heavy wooden gate, inside the log wall surrounding the town, past the rows of thatched huts, toward the sandy open space in the center.

Hernando De Soto, the young Spanish commander, looked down the sandy streets and into the dark doorways of the huts.

A twinge of fear nicked his spine.

Where were the children? The streets were empty, and there was a heavy silence, except for his clanking soldiers.

De Soto looked sideways at the giant Indian chief he had brought along with him from upriver.

Tuskaloosa, called the Black Warrior, stood almost a head taller than the other Indians.

He was dressed in a rich red suit and a red hat, which De Soto had given him, and he strode straight ahead, head high.

There was a polite fiction between the two men that Tuskaloosa was De Soto's guest on the march. But both knew he was a prisoner. They had met upriver on the Alabama, near Line Creek in present-day Montgomery County.

Now they walked the streets of Maubila, the capital of the Maubila Indian tribe. The town probably was located in present-day Clarke County, a few miles southeast of Jackson.

Even though he was only in his middle 30s, De Soto was an old hand at hunting gold in the New World. He had won great distinction as one of Pizarro's lieutenants in Peru, and had gone home to Spain with chests of gold and jewels wrested from the Incas.

Back in the Spanish court, De Soto had chafed at the stately ballet of manners, the bowing and the hand-kissing and the polite talk.

He wanted action. He begged King Charles V for more adventures in America.

The king made him governor of Cuba and gave him a royal license to steal and plunder. De Soto was commissioned to "conquer, pacify and people" the land which is now the southeastern part of the United States.

On his way (he ranged from Florida to Georgia to South Carolina to North Carolina to Tennessee to Alabama) De Soto treated the Indians with exquisite cruelty. He lured the chiefs into meetings with honeyed words, then grabbed and held them hostage. Fight us, he told the Indians, and we'll kill your chief.

He looted the Indian storehouses, and forced the tribes to give him Indian women for his men. Indian slaves carried his baggage.

The Indians caught on. They began telling De Soto of great gold and riches — just over the mountain, in the next town, down the trail a few miles. Just get this Spanish devil out of town.

De Soto and his men fell for the trick. They kept chasing the golden rainbow, over the mountain, down the trail, to the next town.

It is astonishing that the Spaniards could move at all. The soldiers wore armor on the trail, including steel helmets, breastplates, shields and coats of mail — interwoven chips of steel — to turn away the Indian arrows.

His cavaliers, mounted on their horses, were decked out in the cumbersome armor. A pack of bloodhounds was brought along to unloose on the Indians, and greyhounds to chase them when they ran. Along with the drove of pigs, there were cattle and mules tagging along behind the expedition.

Carpenters and gunsmiths and other craftsmen trudged along the trail too, carrying their tools. Some of them specialized in making handcuffs and leg irons for the Indians.

In Montgomery County, Alabama, De Soto was met by Tuskaloosa, the dark-skinned Black Warrior, who offered to take him to the large town of Maubila, in the south. On the way, Tuskaloosa rode a pack horse, and his feet almost dragged the ground.

Now, on a brisk October day of 1540, they had come to Maubila, one of the largest Indian cities in the Southeast. And De Soto was disturbed by the dangerous quiet.

His instincts were right, the flicker of fear was on target. It was an ambush, carefully set up in advance by the giant Indian chief. Inside the Indian huts were thousands of silent warriors, ready to waylay the unsuspecting Spaniards.

Tuskaloosa, who had carefully laid the trap and baited it with stories of gold, talked to De Soto for a moment in the town square, listened to the flutes played by the Indian maidens. Then he suddenly stood up and walked into one of the Indian houses.

By now, a spy had told De Soto of the ambush, and the Spanish commander went to the hut and walked up to Tuskaloosa with smiles and kind words. The giant scornfully turned his back on the Spanish commander.

It may have been a signal.

Suddenly, an Indian warrior leaped out of a doorway and shouted curses down on the Spaniards.

"Robbers! Thieves! Assassins!"

Then he drew back an arrow in his bow.

A Spanish lieutenant, Baltasar de Gallegos, split him open with his sword, and thousands of Indians poured out of the houses, screaming war whoops and thirsting for Spanish blood.

De Soto grouped his men and slowly fought backwards, hacking his way down the sandy streets, now blotched with blood, and out through the gates. There, he mounted a charge by his horsemen, and drove the screaming warriors back inside the gate.

Spanish reinforcements came running, and De Soto mounted an attack on the village. He used cavalry, fresh infantry, and his one artillery piece.

The cannon blew a hole in the wall, and there was wholesale slaughter. Indians were killed by the thousands and some Spaniards were overpowered and killed.

But the Spanish had better guns and swords, and the Indian arrows clattered off the Spanish armor. Soon the town was in flames, and huge clouds of smoke rose over the carnage below.

After nine hours of hacking and shooting, the battle was over. Estimates of the Spanish dead ranged from 20 to 82 soldiers. But estimates of the Indian body count stretched from 2,500 to 11,000. In the beginning, some 600 Spanish soldiers battled at least 10,000 Indians.

The battle destroyed the Maubila Indians as a

power in Alabama. As a minor tribe, they gathered their remnants and limped west of the Tombigbee, toward Mississippi. Later, they moved down closer to Mobile, and gave their name to the bay, the river, the city and the county.

What happened to Tuskaloosa, the giant Black Warrior? He probably was killed in the battle, but his name lives on in Tuscaloosa, home of the University of Alabama and once capital of the state. The Black Warrior River is named for him.

And De Soto? He won a battle at Maubila, but he may have lost his war there. He lost his supplies and baggage, including medicine and books. Worse yet, he lost the wine and wheat necessary for the bread and wine of Catholic mass, and the priests were forced to improvise with a "dry mass," using corn bread.

After licking his wounds in camp for a month, De Soto and his Spaniards headed north, up the Tombigbee, toward present-day Mississippi. He wintered in northern Mississippi, where the warlike Chickasaws dealt him another blow.

In May of 1541, he pushed through the trees and discovered the broad expanse of the Mississippi River, near present-day Memphis, Tenn. His expedition crossed the river and wandered through Arkansas. Then they came back to the great Mississippi again.

Here, on the banks of the Big Muddy, De Soto died of a fever.

His men weighted his body with rocks and buried him in the river, to keep the Indians from finding out about the death of their great leader. The Indians thought De Soto was a god, and it was not good strategy to lose a god.

Under Luis de Moscoso, the 320 survivors built crude boats and floated them down the Mississippi. They finally reached Spanish outposts on the Mexican Gulf coast. On the way, they had to fight off several Indian attacks.

The Battle of Maubila, where De Soto's downhill slide began, probably was the largest land battle ever fought in Alabama.

Although Maubila exists in history, it has escaped archeologists searching for its remains. Nobody knows where Maubila stood.

The remains of the village, along with the bones of the battle, lie undiscovered somewhere along the southern reaches of the Alabama River.

"Now, on a brisk October day of 1540, they had come to Maubila, one of the largest Indian cities in the Southeast. And De Soto was disturbed by the dangerous quiet."

Chapter Three

1704 A. D.

La Femme!
La Femme!
French women come
to Mobile

In the 1600s and 1700s, women and gold decided the fate of North America.

Spain came first, following the voyages of Columbus around 1500. Spanish conquistadors — soldiers of fortune — came clanking in their armor, panting for gold.

Cortes in Mexico, Pizarro in Peru, De Soto in the southeastern U.S. The Spanish adventurers came by the hundreds, eyes gleaming for plunder.

The Spanish established their method of exploration. Find the Indians, sweet talk them, give them baubles, then take their chiefs as hostages. Kill and plunder. Burn the villages, gather up the gold, rape the women, and look around for the next Cibola, the next City of Gold.

The French were gentler. They didn't kill so many Indians. They tried to enslave them, but the Indians faded into the woods when they tired of being slaves. The French came to explore, but more importantly, to trade.

They founded cities on the Gulf Coast — Mobile in 1702, Biloxi in 1717 and New Orleans in 1718. But the French settlements did not flourish, because there were no women.

The French were traders. They bought furs from the Indians, floated them down the rivers, and loaded them aboard the ships for the trip back to France.

But a wandering trader didn't make a very good father, nor a very good settler. Wandering didn't lend itself to family life. On the east coast of America, as the French and Spanish hung onto their sparse settlements on the Gulf, the English came.

The first English ships brought soldiers and explorers, just as the Spanish and French. But the English were more interested in establishing settlements — Jamestown in Virginia, Plymouth in Massachusetts.

There was one important way the English were different. They built houses, they brought farming utensils, and blacksmith tools, and gunsmiths.

They also brought something else.

Women.

The English came to stay. Without children, there would be no settlements. So the English women sailed with their men aboard the ships to America.

The Spanish and the French had a hard time

holding onto their little corners of America, speckled along the Gulf Coast, because they didn't bring women. They tried, but the instinct to wander and explore and trade was too strong.

They founded settlements, but they didn't flourish because they lacked women — and children.

But on the east coast of America — with women, families and children — the English settlements flourished, took root, and grew into a country.

****

The carpenter looked up from the plank he was cutting and peered downstream, down the Mobile River toward the sea, 27 miles away.

In the far distance, just around the bend, he could see the black shapes of the longboats crawling upstream, and the regular sweep of the oars.

He dropped his ax, and yelled. Other workmen came in from the pine woods where they had been making tar and pitch for ships. More men came running from the brickyard.

The people of Fort Louis de la Mobile began to gather on the river bank and the small wooden quay which pushed out into the water.

Official reports of time note that "two French families, with three little girls and seven little boys" lived there. There were 180 men capable of bearing arms, but there were few — if any at all — single women.

Some of the men were living with Indian women. These women, and the Indian boys who served as slaves, followed the men down the muddy streets with the elegant names, the Rue de Bienville, the Rue de Serigny, toward the dock and the approaching boats.

Behind them lay a town of 80 houses, Creole cottages built of cedar or pine and covered with thatched roofs.

The boats came nearer, and the people on the quay could see the soldiers now, their muskets held high over the gunwales of the boats. They could see the helmets of the soldiers in the boats, the sailors pulling at the oars, and some were wearing bonnets.

Bonnets?

"La femme!" shouted the carpenter. Others took up the cry, peering over each other's shoulders at the boats, coming up to the dock. "La femme! La femme!"

The boats pulled alongside the dock, and the grinning sailors held onto the pilings as the two gray-clad nuns shepherded the 23 women ashore.

Each carried a cassette, or a casket, a small box with their belongings inside. Later, they were called the Cassette Girls.

It was July 24, 1704.

Even though he was not there, it was a great day for Jean Baptiste le Moyne, Sieur de Bienville. He and his older brother, Pierre le Moyne, Sieur d'Iberville, sailed from France in 1698 to found a French colony near the mouth of the Mississippi River.

After several false starts, they founded Mobile in 1702, Biloxi in 1717, and Bienville founded New Orleans in 1718.

The first town of Mobile, Fort Louis de la Mobile, was built at Twenty Seven Mile Bluff, near the present site of Mount Vernon, up the Mobile River.

There was the cluster of houses, and a log fort at the center, with six cannon peeping out, a parade ground, a guardhouse, officer's quarters and a chapel. Enlisted men lived in a barracks outside the fort.

Bienville saw that the settlement would die without women and he begged Ponchatrain, the French minister of Marine and Colonies, to send women to Mobile.

From Versailles, from the court of Louis XIV, Ponchatrain wrote to Bienville in America:

"The King is sending to Louisiana (the whole

territory, which included Alabama, was called Louisiana) the vessel *Pelican* commanded by Sieur Du Coudray, a captain of artillery, who is bringing you the regular assistance of the colony.

"By this same ship his Majesty is sending twenty (*most historians believe it was 23*) girls to be married to the Canadians and others who have begun to make themselves a home on the Mobile (River) in order that a colony be firmly established.

"All these girls have been brought up in virtue and piety and know how to work. This will make them very useful to this colony by showing the daughters of the Indians what they can do, and in order that none at all may be sent except those of recognizable and irreproachable virtue his Majesty has directed the Bishop of Quebec to obtain them from places that cannot be suspected of any dissoluteness.

"You will be careful to establish them as best you can and to marry them off to men capable of supporting with some sort of comfort. By the same vessel his Majesty is sending a midwife."

He thought of everything, Ponchatrain did.

A carpenter named Penicaut, aboard another French ship, wrote at the time:

"In fourteen days we reached Fort Mobile, where we found a ship that had arrived from France bringing us food supplies. This ship, named *Le Pelican*, was under the command of M. du Coudray. He had brought 28 (*yet another count, most think it was 23*) girls from France.

"They were the first ones that came to Louisiana. They were quite well-behaved, and so they had no trouble finding husbands."

When the boats landed, and the girls stepped off onto the quay, the men crowded around them, talking and smiling.

There is a story that Madame Langlois, Bienville's cousin (and his housekeeper) helped to marry off the cassette girls.

Within a few weeks, 22 of the girls were married. One, called a "shy maiden," refused all suitors.

Bienville meanwhile returned to Fort Louis from a voyage, and one-day — so the story goes — he heard a noise outside his door.

The 22 newly-married cassette girls were talking, loudly, all at once.

They quickly told him their troubles. They didn't like corn bread and they didn't like grits. They wanted chicken, not venison; veal, not wild turkey; wheat bread, not cornbread.

Give us better food, they laid the ultimatum down, or we go back to France by the next ship.

Madame Langlois came and stood by Bienville. Could she help? She nodded her head.

The women came inside. Madame Langlois taught them how to dry sassafras and mix it with fish, oyster, crab or meat, and make Creole gumbo. The fabled "petticoat rebellion" died among the pungent smells of the cooking pot.

And so the filles de cassette — the cassette girls — melted into Alabama history, and became the founding mothers of Mobile. More filles de cassette came to Alabama. A ship arrived at Dauphin Island in 1717 with 60 more, and more came in 1728.

By this time, floods had driven the French from Twenty Seven Mile Bluff to a spot downriver — the present site of Mobile.

There is some disagreement about the origins of the filles de cassette. Ponchatrain wrote Bienville that all were of "recognizable and irreproachable virtue" and that they had been brought up in "virtue and piety."

Some historians say the cassette girls — some of more than 1,200 women and girls sent to the Gulf Coast colony — came from prisons and insane asylums of France.

Whether they were the prizes of Louis XIV's court or girls taken from the Saltpetriere enclosure on the Seine at Paris — a jail — does not matter now.

What matters is that Bienville's desperate attempt to people a colony by bringing crowds of marriageable women failed.

From the time Mobile was born, the flags of France, Spain, the Republic of Alabama, the Confederate States of America and Old Glory have flown over the city.

And under each flag, the descendants of the filles de cassette, those cassette girls who stepped out of those longboats that day in 1704, have lived and died, and are buried in the sandy-loamed history of Mobile.

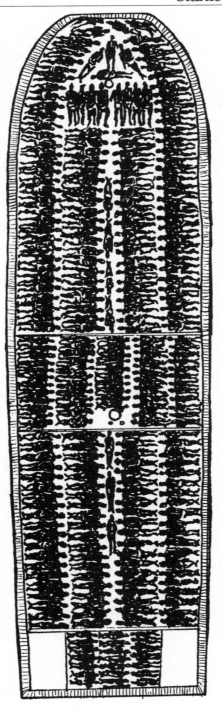

Chapter Four

1721 A. D.

Alabama's first slave ship: The *Africaine* drops anchor at Mobile

Jean Baptiste Le Moyne, Sieur de Bienville, French governor at Mobile, looked out on the rich bottom land near the town.

The underbrush grew quickly, reaching up for the lower limbs of the trees, and it panged Bienville's heart to see the rich fields unused. In his mind's eye, he could see fields of rice and indigo and corn, and he knew that tilled fields meant a stable colony.

Bienville had heard about the English, settling on the Atlantic seaboard. English brought their wives, and their children. They had come to stay.

But Bienville's Frenchmen found relaxation with Indian women, and seemed more interested in gathering furs than tilling the land. Bienville tried to enslave the Indians, tried to make them plow the land, but the Indians caught on, and melted into the forests when the Frenchmen came looking for slaves.

Bienville, who helped found Mobile in 1702, wrote back home to France:

How about us capturing some Indians, and sending them to the West Indies, and there swapping them for black slaves? Won't work, came the answer from a French minister, the people in the West Indies would not part with their valuable black slaves for worthless Indians.

All right, said Bienville, let's get some black slaves in here. We've got to start working the land, or this colony will die.

On March 17, 1721, a French ship of war, the *Africaine*, dropped anchor in Mobile Bay. It was the first slave ship to unload in Alabama.

Chains clanked, and the black figures came up on deck, out of the deadly hold. A total of 120 black people stepped out of the boats onto the shores of Mobile Bay. *Africaine* had loaded 224 slaves aboard on the Guinea coast of Africa, and more than 100 had died in the terrible 'Middle Passage.'

The black slaves worked the fields, and more slave ships came. *Neride*, with 238 more. The Western, or Indian Company, brought slaves to Alabama and sold them for 660 livres ($176) apiece.

The slaves worked the land, and helped to grow the rice and indigo, and the colony flourished. By 1734, the colonists were making money from the farming, and the price of a slave had gone to 1,400 livres, more than $350.

By 1746, there were 4,730 slaves in Alabama, and by the 1760s, when the French turned over Mobile to the British, there were about 6,000 slaves in the state.

Under the French, the slaves were governed by an edict from the King of France, issued in 1724 and called the "Black Code." It provided, among other things: Slaves could not own property, and they couldn't vote. Husbands and wives were not to be sold separately if they belonged to the same master, and children under 14 were not to be separated from their parents.

The code was rough on runaway slaves. If a slave ran, and stayed gone for more than a month, and was recaptured, the iron law said his ears would be cut off, and that he would be branded with the fleur de luce on the shoulder.

If he ran away again, he would be hamstrung, his Achilles tendon would be cut.

Alabama was French, then British, then became a part of the U.S. in the early 1800s, and cotton was the money crop of the farmers. More slaves, more cotton, and the great plantations flourished.

The plantation owners were afraid of education. After the Nat Turner slave rebellion in Virginia in the early 1830s, the Alabama General Assembly made it against the law to teach black people to read. Maximum fine: $500.

Marriages between slaves had no legal status, but most masters respected them. Most plantation owners preferred their slaves to marry on the plantation, but there were records of marriages between plantations.

In 1862, one S.J. Chapman of Eutaw wrote to a Mrs. Walton of Strawberry Hill plantation:

"My valet de chambre — Jeff — having formed an attachment for Miss Abbey your servant, and being solicitous of entering into a matrimonial alliance with his dulcinea, requests me to write a recommendation to you, bespeaking for him your favorable consideration of his application to wed Miss Abbey.

"Hoping that you will sanction Miss Abbey's choice and allow these sable children of Africa to unite their destinies in the silken tie of Hymen, with consideration, I am very respectfully..."

In the slave record at Strawberry Hill, there is a notation that Jeff and Abbey were married in 1852. And, of course, if they lived until 1865 — the end of the Civil War — they became free.

Slavery, by its very nature, was brutal. But there was affection among the brutalities. Harry Toulmin of Washington County, writing his will in 1823, said:

"It has long been my intention to emancipate Toney (a slave)...I do not wish to petition our Alabama Assembly about his emancipation...I scorn to petition for what I believe to be a right. Let him be sent with proper passport (to freedom)."

Mobile was the center of slave trading during the early years of the state's history. The market in Mobile was on the west side of Royal Street, between St. Louis and St. Frances. The slave barracks was a three-story brick building with barred windows.

After 1840, Montgomery became the state's chief slave market. Here, some dealers kept individual depots where slaves were kept for sale.

One newspaper correspondent said he saw 20 different lots sold "at the fountain" in one day of 1860.

There were slave-running rings, bandits who stole slaves in Florida and ran them into Alabama to sell.

The free black people — and there were more than 2,500 *free* black people in Alabama in 1860 — had to look out for the slave-runners.

There is the case of Amy Butcher and her daughter Caty of Prince George County, Virginia. Both were free blacks. They were kidnapped and brought to Alabama.

They filed suit for their freedom in Madison County in 1818, and respectable witnesses said they were free citizens of Virginia. But the case was continued, year after year, and finally the two women gave up and sank back into slavery.

Though it was hard to do under Alabama law, masters continued to free slaves. Sometimes free black men married slave women, buying them from their masters.

Two slaves in Tuscaloosa, Charles Addison and a man named Luffborough, bought themselves and their families and went back to Africa. They sailed to Liberia.

When Gen. Robert E. Lee sent the rider with the white flag out across the field at Appomattox, the death knell was rung for slavery.

Freedom was glorious to some of the slaves, confusing to others. Some slaves shouted their "hallelujahs" and scattered to the winds in their new-found freedom, some drifted to the cities.

Many of the slaves, offered a chance to stay on as tenants on their home plantations, stayed where they were.

They felt they had no place else to go.

Chapter Five

1776 A. D.

Just before the Revolution: Mobile is a haven for Tories

Thomas Bassett, a refugee, sat in the longboat and looked back at the ship which had brought him from Georgia.

The ship, a British merchantman, lay at anchor in the sheltered roadstead at Dauphin Island, just inside Mobile Bay.

Up the bay were the cupolas, the sentry boxes, the guns, of Fort Charlotte and the low-lying cottages of

Mobile.

Bassett was a Tory who thought the rebel non-sense about independence was just that — nonsense. Worse, it was treason.

Back home on his plantation in Georgia, the rebels had badgered him. They had killed his stock, ruined his crops, shouted obscenities at him and his family when they went to town. Finally Bassett could stand it no more. He would go to a new place, a place where he could be loyal to king and country, and raise his family in peace, and make a living.

He sold his plantation in Georgia, at a big loss. He packed his gear, gathered his family around him, and left Georgia — a refugee from American independence.

But he was not the usual refugee. He was well-dressed, with coat and ruffled shirt. Back in the longboat, his wife and two children watched the sailors put their back into the oars.

In a second longboat were 14 black people, all belonging to Bassett. He was on his way to a new life in Alabama, but it would not necessarily be a hard life. He had money, and slaves.

Most importantly, he had land.

Peter Chester, the British governor of West Florida at Pensacola, had an idea how he would populate the area with Tories — people loyal to the British king.

He would take the Tories fleeing from the eastern seaboard — loyalists chased out of Georgia, the Carolinas, Virginia, Maryland, even Pennsylvania and New York, and give them land upriver from Mobile.

That way, the king would populate the new frontier with loyal subjects.

In his pocket, Bassett had a land patent signed by Chester. He now owned 200 acres of land on the river, a quarter mile up from McIntosh Bluff, and 750 more acres nearby.

It was enough, he nodded to himself as the longboat crunched into the King's Wharf, stretching out from the walls of Fort Charlotte. It was enough to make a new life.

Soon he and his family and his slaves would step into the longboats again for the trip upriver, and the new life — hard at first, more comfortable later — would begin.

It was June 21, 1776. In 13 days — on July 4, 1776 — they would sign the Declaration of Independence in Philadelphia and the fever of freedom would sweep the eastern seaboard.

But on this day in June of 1776, Bassett and his family looked out on British Mobile. The fort, eight-pounders peeping through the masonry walls, stretched up on the left, and a lonely sentry walked the wall, outlined against the evening sky.

Bassett was warned about the fort. Stay away from it, they had told him in Pensacola; it's a pest hole. Soldiers dying all the time. There was putrid bilious fever (yellow fever), flux (dysentery), jail fever (typhus) and typhoid, plus cases of malaria.

The Bassetts gave the fort a wide berth, moving up Royal Street to an inn, as the slaves hoisted their baggage. They passed the French-style cottages, cypress logs and whitewashed walls.

Later, they walked the sandy streets to the westernmost edge of town, only three short blocks from the river. Here, they saw the wooden pavilions where the Indian congresses were held, and the swampy pine scrub stretching into the distance.

The French had settled Mobile, and there were French families living there in 1776, and French plantation owners upriver and across the bay.

The British had come into Mobile in 1763, after the Treaty of Paris, when France turned over its Gulf Coast possessions to the British.

Maj. Robert Farmar, 45 years old, career British army, came on Oct. 20, 1763, to take possession.

The treaty stipulated that the British only take

possession of the fort, that the private property and the French residents were not to be molested.

With these kid-gloves rules, the British soon found themselves renting a house for a hospital, among other things.

The British colony of West Florida ran from the Chattahoochee River (now the dividing line between Georgia and Alabama) to the Mississippi River. The northern boundary ran along the 31st parallel (on a east-west line with present-day Mount Vernon), but the British moved it farther north later.

Farmar, who came from Jamaica, landed with a proclamation (in French, for most of the inhabitants of Mobile were French), which said that the people were now "subject to the Laws of England, by which they shall be peacefully protected in their rights and properties."

It also said: "Those among the French inhabitants who shall choose to remain in their diverse abodes and live under the laws of England and his Britannic Majesty's government, as soon as may be possible shall repair to Mobile there to take oath of allegiance.

"Those who will not (sign the oath of allegiance) within three months . . . shall be dispossessed and compelled to quit this portion of the country ceded to the English nation."

About 350 people lived in Mobile in 1763. By April 1764, only eight people had signed the oath of allegiance to the British crown. Many French settlers sold their land and moved to New Orleans. But they found the Spanish (who controlled New Orleans) to be unfriendly, and many soon returned to Mobile.

The first British governor of West Florida was a hot-headed Scot named George Johnstone. He had lately tried to challenge a newspaper editor in England to a duel, for some slight, and had wound up in a fist fight with him.

He brought his hot temper to Mobile, and quarreled with everybody in sight. He and Farmar squabbled over civil authority versus military authority, and Johnstone had real trouble enforcing the Stamp Act.

While under British rule, the colony was ruled by a governor, appointed by the king, by a Council (a sort of Senate) of 12 people nominated by the governor, and a lower house (an Assembly) elected by the free holders of the colony.

Johnstone continually had trouble with the Assembly, refusing to call a meeting until he had been in the colony a year and a half.

But he had better luck with the Indians. He and John Stuart, the English Superintendent of Indian Affairs, had a series of congresses with the leaders of the main tribes.

The Creeks came down to Pensacola for the meeting, and the Choctaws and Chickasaws gathered in Mobile.

Toward the end of the congress, the chief of the Choctaws, Mingo Huma, arose.

"The medal which I wear was given to me by the French governor as a token of power and authority to govern my people but he . . . has gone away and left me destitute. I am sensible it is impossible for a child to have two fathers; I now acknowledge you to be my father, in token of which I deliver you my (French) commission and medal. I hope you will replace them with others as good and honorable."

Johnstone served until 1769, to be succeeded by Gov. John Eliot. Eliot arrived in Pensacola, took the oath as governor on April 2, 1769, and promptly committed suicide. Some said his lady loved another man.

Then came Montfort Browne, the lieutenant who had opposed Johnstone in the Assembly. Browne was as cantankerous as Johnstone had been.

The last of the British governors, Peter Chester, was appointed in 1770 and served until 1780.

Under Chester's friendly hand, West Florida became a haven for Tories — British loyalists — from the eastern states.

Most refugees wound up with land on Mobile Bay, the Tensaw and Tombigbee rivers, or streams that fed into them.

Soon there was a large nest of loyal British subjects, fervent Tories, gathered around Mobile.

When Capt. James Willing came to the Tensaw settlement and read the Declaration of Independence in 1778, they were unfriendly. They threw Willing into a dungeon at Fort Charlotte and called him a traitor.

Two of the ablest leaders were attacked by their neighbors. Major Farmar was court martialed, charged with taking money meant for the Indians. But he was acquitted, and retired to his plantation across the bay.

Chester himself was attacked by members of the Assembly. Some 130 leading citizens — about half from Mobile — asked for his removal. But, probably because of his success in transplanting Tories, the king let him stay.

Mobile was truly a pest hole. Soldiers stationed at Fort Charlotte were continually getting sick and dying off. Fevers and dysentery decimated the garrison, regularly.

"Mobile must be the most unhealthy place on the face of the earth," wrote Governor Johnstone, and he warned that "persisting in quartering troops there is a kind of war against Heaven, by the piling up of dead bodies."

A Swiss mercenary, Brig. Gen. Frederick Haldimand, arrived in 1767 to command the British troops, and he tried to make changes. He moved the palisade further from the barracks to allow for fresh air, and he began to work on a new hospital. He tried to dig new wells, trying to find healthier water.

Haldimand thought of invading the Spanish port of New Orleans, to enlarge the British base on the Gulf.

But in New Orleans, a young Spaniard named

Bernardo de Galvez had different ideas. He thought of invading Mobile.

Chapter Six

1780 A. D.

The Spanish take Mobile from the English

The year was 1780, and the curtain was closing on the drama of the American Revolution.

Sir Henry Clinton and his redcoats were penned in New York by George Washington and his ragged Americans, and British Gen. Charles Cornwallis was sweeping through Georgia and South Carolina, heading northward toward Yorktown and disaster and "The World Turned Upside Down."

Then, on June 21, 1779, there came a little-known development which became important to Alabama:

Spain declared war on Britain, coming down on the side of the American independence.

While the Revolutionary War drama was unfolding on the eastern seaboard, British West Florida stood solidly with George III, the Tories in control. The British flag fluttered over Pensacola and Mobile's Fort Charlotte.

In New Orleans, held by the Spanish, the young governor was Bernardo de Galvez . He received word that his country was at war with Britain. He turned his eyes eastward, toward Fort Charlotte at Mobile and the capital of West Florida, Pensacola.

At 33, Galvez was the youngest governor Spanish Louisiana had seen. A portly young man, he was ambitious and energetic. He immediately asked Havana for help in raising an invasion force to attack Mobile and Pensacola.

After taking some British strongpoints in Mississippi, Galvez marshaled 1,400 men and a squadron of transport ships and set sail for Mobile in February 1780.

Bucking hurricane-strength winds, he reached Mobile Bay by the end of February. Several of his ships were blown aground on the sandbar across the bay entrance, but Galvez put his men to work, and pulled the ships off the sand.

Fort Charlotte, the strongpoint at Mobile, was built by the French in 1717 near the bay at the lower end of the town. When the British took it over, they changed its name from Fort Conde — so named by the French — to Fort Charlotte, for the British queen.

The British mounted more than 30 cannon along the walls of the fort.

Inside the fort was British Capt. Elias Durnford, an army engineer and former lieutenant governor of West Florida.

Galvez landed his ships, unloaded the artillery from them, and set up positions above the town. Then he sent Capt. Francisco Bouligny into the fort under a white flag to talk to Durnford. Bouligny and Durnford were old friends.

Durnford and Bouligny dined together, raised glasses to their respective kings. Bouligny told his friend that Galvez had 2,500 men, and really, to minimize the loss of life, he should surrender.

No, Durnford shook his head. He had heard that the Spanish invasion force had been heavily damaged by the high winds, and Indian spies told him that many of the soldiers in Galvez's army were untrained militia.

From this point, the siege became a battle of manners, a chivalrous ballet of civilized behavior, while the guns bristled in the background.

Galvez intercepted a letter from British Governor John Campbell in Pensacola, notifying Durnford that he was sending 500 British soldiers to his relief. Galvez read the letter and looked again at the fort, the guns peeping through the wall. He must move, and move now, before the British reinforcements arrived from Pensacola.

Inside the brick and masonry walls, Durnford called his men together. In a letter, he wrote: "(I) told them that if any man among them was afraid to stand by me, that I should open the gate and he should freely pass. This had the desired effect, and not a man moved. I then read to them my answer to the summons (a Galvez request to surrender), in which they all joined in three cheers..."

Meanwhile, Durnford burned some houses near the fort, to clear the line of fire between the fort and the Spanish emplacements.

Then he sent some men out under a white flag. They presented to Galvez a dozen bottles of wine, a dozen chickens, a dozen loaves of bread, a mutton, and some other provisions for some English prisoners.

Not to be outdone, Galvez sent Durnford a case of Bordeaux wine, another case of Spanish wine, a box of

citrons and oranges, a box of tea biscuits, and a box of
Havana cigars. The prisoners were being treated well,
he told Durnford.

Then Galvez apologized for having to introduce a
harsh note into this civilized discourse, and offered a
"small reproach." He regretted that military necessity
had forced Durnford to burn the houses. "Fortresses
are constructed solely to defend towns, but you are
commencing to destroy the town in favor of a fortress
incapable of defense."

For the sake of the poor citizens of Mobile, Galvez
was willing to promise not to put any of his guns behind
houses, if Durnford would stop burning the houses.

Back and forth the polite message went, always
courteous, always solicitous, but with the threat of the
booming guns lying just behind the language.

Between letters, Galvez feinted this way and that,
but always moving his artillery closer to the fort. He
knew he had to move now, the reinforcements for the
British were on the march from Pensacola.

Finally the Spanish guns were moved close in to
the fort, and Durnford looked over the wall. He shook
his head. He was outnumbered seven to one, the
Spanish guns would crumble his fort, it was useless.

The white flag came out of the fort again, this time
to negotiate for the surrender.

On the outside looking in, Galvez was desperate.
His Indian spies reported to him that there were more
than 1,000 English troops in the Tensaw district, just
above Mobile. It was now or never.

At 10 a.m. on the morning of March 10, 1780,
Durnford turned over the fort to Galvez. Durnford
described the scene in a letter to his superiors.

"It is my misfortune to inform you that this morning my small but brave garrison marched down the
breach, and surrendered themselves prisoners of war
to General Bernardo de Galvez's superior arms. I write
for your information and request that you will do me

the favor to inform Mrs. Durnford that I am in good health and that she ought to be under no uneasiness in my fate. When it is in my power to send you the capitulation and state precedent for it...I will do it; in the meantime I assure you sir, that no man in the garrison hath stained the lustre of British arms..."

As a reward for the capture of Mobile, Galvez was made field marshal in command of all Spanish operations in America and wore the title: "Governor of Louisiana and Mobile."

He immediately launched plans to take Pensacola. A Spanish force moved overland to attack it by land, and Galvez mounted another invading force from the sea. Again, Galvez was successful. He took Pensacola in May of 1781, and British West Florida belonged to the Spanish.

Later, in 1795, Spain and the United States worked out a line (called Ellicott's Line) separating American and Spanish territory. It ran along the 31st parallel through Mt. Vernon, and, to the consternation of the Spanish, it left St. Stephens inside the American sector.

In the War of 1812, the Spanish allowed the British to use the port of Mobile to stir up the Indians against the Americans. On April 5, 1813, Gen. James Wilkinson led an American force in an attack on Spanish Mobile, and took the city.

It was the first time the Stars and Stripes had flown over the whole state of Alabama.

After his successful invasions of Mobile and Pensacola, Bernardo de Galvez became a Spanish military hero, and served as field marshal of Spanish forces and viceroy of New Spain.

He died in 1786, at the age of 40, in Mexico City.

Chapter Seven

1781 A. D.

Alabama Revolutionary War battle: Spanish fight British at Mobile

The fog was thick, hugging the ground in a close embrace, and Spanish Sublieutenant Manuel de Cordoba squinted as he tried to see out the window of the fort.

He saw black shapes flitting through the gray shrouds of mist, and he looked closer. There were men out there, moving. Their black figures flickered in and out of his vision.

He nodded. They were militia — black volunteers from New Orleans serving in the Spanish Army — returning from outer trenches of the Spanish fort on Mobile Bay's east shore.

The black figures came closer; through a rift in the fog, he saw the red coats of the soldiers, closing in on the house. There was a shout of alarm, a rifle shot, then a spattering of fire.

These were British troops, not Spanish. Cordoba's eyes widened, and he shouted amongst the din. But it was too late, the British had infiltrated the outer line of Spanish trenches. Heavy firing began, and the screams of battle followed.

For his mistake, Cordoba would die.

It was Jan. 7, 1781, and the bloodiest battle of the Revolutionary War in Alabama was beginning.

Ironically, the battle was fought by the British, Spanish, Germans, Indians and black militiamen from New Orleans fighting for the Spanish — but there were no Americans.

The battle was waged at a place about eight miles east of Mobile, near the present Spanish Fort. The French called it the French Village, the Spanish called it La Aldea (the Village).

When Washington was pushing Cornwallis toward Yorktown (the British surrendered there on Oct. 19, 1781), another war was being waged on the Gulf Coast. Britain held Pensacola, the capital of West Florida. The Spanish, under Galvez, held Mobile. In March 1781, Galvez had taken Mobile from the British. The Americans and the Spanish were allies, Spain having declared war on Britain.

To protect Mobile from the British, Galvez ordered that La Aldea, The Village, be fortified. If the British came overland from Pensacola, they first would have to take this point, before moving across the bay on

Mobile.

Trenches were dug at The Village, and sharpened stakes were driven into the ground. The Spanish troops — infantrymen from the line regiments of Principe, Espana, Navarra and Havana — cleaned muskets and waited. In the outer trenches, black troops — who had showed great bravery in the Louisiana campaign of Galvez — watched the edge of the woods.

They were members of the Company of Free Mulatto Militia, formed by Galvez in New Orleans, and some had fought with Galvez when he took Mobile, 10 months earlier.

Gen. John Campbell, in command of British forces in Pensacola, was determined to harass the Spanish at Mobile. During the winter of 1780-81, he sent three attacks against Spanish outposts in the area, including The Village.

Col. Jose de Ezpeleta, the Spanish commander at Mobile's Fort Charlotte, sent an urgent call to Galvez for help.

From Havana, Galvez sent eight ships and 500 men, but the ships — for some reason — could not enter Mobile Bay, and turned westward toward the mouth of the Mississippi River, where they landed at the pilot station of Belize.

Ezpeleta needed these troops for the defense of Mobile, but they were far away when he needed them.

At The Village, Ezpeleta maintained a garrison of 190 men. His orders: Protect the approaches to Mobile.

Late in December, Campbell gathered a force in Pensacola to attack The Village. There were 60 Waldeckers, German troops hired by George III to fight against the American revolutionaries — and the Spanish.

There were Indians, 2,000 of them in Pensacola, who had volunteered to fight against the Spanish, but Campbell put little faith in their fighting ability.

There were West Florida Royal Foresters, mounted

Loyalist settlers who worked closely with the Indians in raids along the exposed Spanish frontier. Some 250 Tories from Maryland and Pennsylvania accompanied the raiding party.

And there were British regulars, about 100 soldiers from 60th (Royal American) Regiment of Foot.

This collection of regular British infantry, Tory settlers, Indians and German mercenaries set out from Pensacola on Jan. 3, 1781. They were commanded by Col. J. L. W. Hanxleden of the Waldeck Regiment.

Meanwhile, three British ships used a trick to slip past Spanish guns at the mouth of Mobile Bay. Captain Deans of a frigate ordered the British colors hidden and he flew some Spanish banners they had captured.

The Spanish gunners waved in friendship as the British ships moved past their guns and into the bay on Jan. 5, 1781.

The fourth attack on The Village was the best organized. With some 200 white soldiers and from 200 to 500 Indians, Hanxleden brought two four-pounder field pieces with him.

At dawn on Jan. 7, through the thick fog, the British troops moved stealthily through the camp of the black militia troops from New Orleans.

Sublieutenant Cordoba saw the black shapes gliding through the fog, waited too long to sound the alarm, and British fire killed him immediately.

The Spanish troops, though surprised, recovered quickly and opened fire. It was a close-range battle, with soldiers lunging at each other with bayonets and knives.

"Viva El Rey," shouted the Spanish soldiers, and the British answered in kind: "Long Live the King."

The Waldeckers had plunged ahead of the other troops. They scurried into the Spanish trenches, looking for safety. Instead, they found death, and most of them died in the trenches.

After the first assault, Hanxleden halted his troops

and sent out parties to the flanks of the Spanish position, thrusting for weak spots.

Meanwhile, Spanish sharpshooters raked the British positions with deadly, accurate fire.

"Our men, who had resolved to sell their lives dearly," wrote Ezpeleta, "opened a general volley against the enemy."

The Waldeck sergeant major, the commander's son, wildly charged the Spanish grenadiers with his troops, shouting, "Viva George Third!" He was impaled on a Spanish bayonet.

One of the British attackers was a man named William Augustus Bowles, a Maryland Loyalist who had a disagreement with his superior officer and left the unit in disgust.

Bowles had joined the Creek Indians in Florida as one of their principal warriors. He dressed like an Indian, cut his hair in the Indian manner, he became an Indian. Later, he would become Director General of the Muskogee (Muscogee or Creek) Nation after the Revolutionary War.

One of Bowles' fellow soldiers tells of his friend's bravery at The Village:

"In the midst of all this danger, Bowles, with the coolness of an unconcerned spectator, very leisurely loaded and discharged his rifle gun at those who were firing from the windows (of the palisade); and when the British soldiers called to the ... officers to save their lives by flight, our hero posted himself behind a tree, within a few yards of the (breast) work, loading and firing alone; and he must undoubtedly have been killed or taken, had not a cannonball shivered the tree to pieces and driven him unhurt, to gain the small flying party, already at the distance of a quarter of a mile."

In the attack, Col. Hanxleden had been killed and Philip B. Key, captain of the combined Maryland-Pennsylvania Loyalists, assumed command of the British force.

Some Spanish militia ran with the first onslaught of the British. They ran toward the bay, hoping to escape in a boat which had brought rations from Mobile the afternoon before.

The boat was gone, however, and the terrified militiamen were caught in the middle of a fire fight between the British and Spanish positions. They fought bravely, but one historian reasons that their bravery was based in fear: They were afraid of being scalped by the Indians.

Casualties were heavy on both sides. The Spanish counted several bodies in the trenches and behind the palisades, and three more bodies were discovered along the path of the British retreat. Col. Hanxleden lay dead at the foot of the palisade.

In all, the Spanish defenders at The Village lost a third of their force, 14 killed, 23 wounded; one man lost as a prisoner.

The British licked their wounds on the way back to Pensacola. They suffered an estimated 18 dead and at least 60 wounded, plus at least two dead Indians and five wounded. Total British casualties: 85.

After the Battle of The Village, Mobile was safe. Pensacola would soon fall to Galvez's invading army, a blow which would take away the Gulf Coast from the British and contribute to their final defeat in the Revolutionary War.

++++++++++++++++++

(Note: Research on this story was done by Jack D. L. Holmes, former professor of history at the University of Alabama at Birmingham. An expert on Spanish activities in Alabama, Dr. Holmes spent years gathering material about this battle, searching archives in Spain and others of Europe, and was knighted by the Spanish government for his work. His paper, "Bloodiest Day of the American Revolution: Counter Attack at The

Village, Jan. 7, 1781," was read at the Alabama Academy of Science in Mobile April 8-10, 1976.)

Chapter Eight

1790 A. D.

The emperor of the Creeks in Alabama: Alexander McGillivray or Hoboi-Hili-Miko?

From his hiding place behind the bales of cotton, the American secret agent watched the Spanish sloop slide easily alongside the New York dock, and the deck hands tossed over the mooring lines.

There was the usual port routine: The Spanish captain talked with American port authorities, papers were signed, all went to the captain's cabin for a drink, and the Spanish sailors trooped across the gangplank for a night on th town.

But the American secret agent stayed where he was, hunkered behind the cotton bales on the dock. Then a tall Spaniard wearing a black greatcloak came up on deck. He was carrying a leather bag, and he looked up and down the dock beforehe walked down the gangplank.

The American agent nodded his head and smiled. This was his man. Keeping a safe distance, he followed the Spaniard down the dock and into the Manhattan traffic — carriages, dray wagons, men on horseback, pedestrians.

The year was 1790, and New York was the capital of the fledgling country. George Washington, serving his first term as President, was trying to keep his head above water.

European countries were sniping at the brand new country. England, still smarting over her defeat in the Revolutionary War, was looking for a chance to bite back, and Spain held Pensacola, Mobile and New Orleans.

And the Indians along the American frontier were unfriendly and ready for war.

In a tavern meeting room near the Battery, Washington was trying to solve the Indian problem. He had invited a crowd of Indian chiefs from the southern frontier to work out a peace treaty.

The greatest chief among them was a tall (6-2) man with dark hair and bold piercing eyes. The Indians called him Hoboi-Hili-Miko, the Good Child King, but the Americans called him Alexander McGillivray.

McGillivray called himself Emperor of the Creeks (or Muscogees) and he lived in an Indian town on the Coosa River, near present-day Wetumpka.

Now, McGillivray and the other chiefs were conferring with Henry Knox, once Washington's artillery general during the War, now serving as Secretary of War.

The Spanish agent — the tall man who had walked off the gangplank alone — held his ever-present leather bag close, and watched the Indians file into the tavern to meet with Knox.

The Spaniard's bag was full of gold, and the agent wanted to give it to McGillivray, hoping to bribe away any chance for a peaceful treaty with the U.S.

But the American agent stayed close to the Spanish agent with the bag of gold, and made sure he did not get within talking distance of McGillivray.

Toward the end of the summer, the treaty was concluded: Peace between the Creeks and the U.S. The Creeks and Seminoles would be under the protection of the U.S. and would not make any treaties with any other nation. And the Creeks gave up claims they had to lands in Georgia.

So, most people thought, Washington had bagged McGillivray, had bested the wily chief in negotiation.

But no, there was a secret treaty which was not announced. It said that the Creeks, in two years, would begin trading with the Americans. The treaty also appointed McGillivray to the rank of brigadier general in the U.S. Army, with a yearly salary of $1,200, and it gave his fellow chiefs salaries from the U.S.

McGillivray must have laughed. At the same time, he was holding a commission — and drawing a salary — from the Spanish. Serving two masters? McGillivray once shrugged: An Indian should not be expected to refuse any gift offered to him. And so, after the treaty in New York, McGillivray came back to Alabama and continued his secret negotiations with the Spanish authorities in Pensacola.

And his Creek nation was strengthened; it had additional prestige and power because of McGillivray's negotiating skill.

The story of Alexander McGillivray began when

his father — a 16-year-old Scot boy — arrived in America, looking for his fortune. On a trading trip into the Indian country out of Charleston, the boy helped with the pack horses, and was given a pocket knife for his trouble.

The boy, Lachlan McGillivray, traded the pocket knife to the Indians for deer skins, and took them back to the coast.

From his pocket knife beginning, Lachlan McGillivray built a fortune trading with Indians. He soon owned two plantations in Georgia, and became a rich man.

On a trading trip into Alabama, Lachlan McGillivray saw a beautiful young Indian princess named Sehoy Marchand. She was sixteen, with curly black hair and laughing eyes, and he fell in love with her.

She was the daughter of Captain Marchand, a Frenchman who once commanded Fort Toulouse on the Coosa. Her mother was a princess, a member of the ruling Wind clan of the Creeks.

Lachlan McGillivray married his Indian princess, and a son was born at the Apple Grove, or Little Tallassee, near Wetumpka. The son, Alexander McGillivray, played with Indian boys, and hunted and fished up and down the Coosa.

He went to Charleston as a teenager to learn about the big world beyond the Indian villages. He learned the social graces of the whites, how to bow and smile and make polite conversation.

When the Revolutionary War began, he and his father fought with the British against the Americans, and it was the losing side.

The winning Americans stripped Lachlan McGillivray of his plantations, and the old man went back to Scotland to live out his days.

But his son, with his knowledge of white ways and his great charm, became the great chief of the Creeks.

With this treaty and that, now siding with the Spanish, now cozying up to the Americans, McGillivray kept everybody off balance. And his beloved Creeks grew in stature and prestige.

When McGillivray appeared on the scene at the great Indian city near Wetumpka, the Creeks were disorganized, in disarray, under attack from several different directions.

McGillivray consolidated them, united them, got them going in the same direction. At the height of his power, he welded them into a powerful force in the American south.

But, even as a young man, McGillivray had health problems.

It was Feb. 17, 1793, when McGillivray lay sick in a friend's home in Pensacola. Sick with the gout and pneumonia, he sank into a coma and died in the arms of his old friend and partner, the Scot trader Panton. He was only 33.

After he was gone, the Creeks looked for another great leader, another MicGillivray, another Hoboi-Hili-Miko. But there was no one, no one who could see the broad picture, no one with the leadership to deal with the whites and Indians with knowledge and skill.

Leaderless, the Creeks and other Indians soon trod the "Trail of Tears," the path from their homelands in Georgia and Alabama into exile in Oklahoma, and their lands were grabbed by the Americans.

With his death went the last chance the Indians had of keeping their lands. There were abandoned, leaderless, unequipped to handle the horde of land-hungry whites, and the road to exile stretched before them.

Chapter Nine

1803 A. D.

Reform! He shouted: They laughed, and named the town

In the early 1800s, the settlements in Alabama were as rough as a corn cob. It was the frontier, where living was backbreaking hard and death came as easy as the swish-thunk of an Indian tomahawk in the night.

The first men moving west were the ne'er-do-wells, the rejects of the American society on the eastern seaboard. Joining the second sons, who would never inherit, were wenches who felt more at home raising a glass in a tavern than standing over a washpot outside a frontier farmhouse.

A preacher brave enough to point out the sinful ways of the settlers had to watch his step, or he might get a free ride out of town on a rail.

In 1790, a Baptist minister rowed across the Tombigbee River with high hopes of saving some of the lost souls at wicked St. Stephens. Just as quick, he was rowed back across the river and promised a generous coat of tar and feathers if he came back. He didn't come back.

But in 1803, a Connecticut-born Methodist minister named Lorenzo Dow stood on the porch of a Georgia house and looked to the west. There were souls to save out there in those settlements, and he was the man God had chosen to save them.

Friends gave him a pass from the governor of Georgia, a good horse, a warm cloak, a watch, and $53.

Thus armed against the devil, Dow set out into the Alabama and Mississippi wilderness. He was the first Protestant minister to preach in the area which was later to become Alabama.

He forded rivers, stayed with half-blood Indians, held camp meetings in the settlements, and rode his horse through swamp and thicket, looking for the next soul to save.

At St. Stephens (Alabama's first capital, located in Washington County), his visit interrupted the boisterous fun of the drunken settlers, and they invited him to leave.

As he swung onto his horse and headed for Mississippi, he raised his hand and prayed to God to send a curse upon the place. One day, he said, no stone would lie atop another, and the settlement would become a roosting place for bats and owls.

Sure enough, the life of St. Stephens ebbed and flowed. It became the state's first territorial capital, and then it slowly sank into oblivion. It was a dead city, marked only by crumbling chimneys, by the 1860s. A roosting place for bats and owls.

Dow pushed on through the Choctaw Nation, moving due west.

By this time, his money pouch was getting light. In Sixtown of the Choctaw Nation, he traded his saddle blanket for corn, to feed his horse. Better saddle sores than an empty belly, he must have figured.

But he was received with hospitality at the Natchez settlement on the Mississippi River, and Dow — after some hard preaching — headed back to Georgia.

He had to get another horse. He sold his watch to pay expenses. He wore out his pantaloons and for the last few hundred miles, he traveled without shoes or outer garment. He had sold his cloak.

When he arrived back in Georgia, he had traveled 4,000 miles in less than seven months. He was exhausted and broke, but he proved his philosophy by declining many offers of money and handsome presents. He accepted only those things he needed to fulfill his engagements, nothing else.

In 1804, he courted and married Peggy Miller of Connecticut (he called her his "rib") and she traveled with him through the wilds of the Southeast for a time.

One of his main problems was the group of rowdies in the settlements. Drunk on Demon Rum, they sometimes dropped burning brimstone down the chimneys of the meeting houses, the log churches.

But Dow knew how to handle them. One group of bullies threatened not only to break up the meeting, but to lynch Dow. He went to them, with Peggy on his arm. Soon he won over the leader and several others, and they escorted the Dows back to camp.

Dow, who sometimes called himself Crazy Dow, was respected by the rawboned citizens of the frontier. Beyond being a preacher, he was a sort of mystical doctor to some of them.

Once, Dow was roused from his bed in a tavern by a landlord, who explained that one of the men in the barroom below had lost his purse. Dow came down the stairs and looked into the hostile faces.

"Bring me your large dinner pot," he ordered the landlord, "and bring me the old red cock from the roost."

There was a flutter of wings and soot in the air. Then Dow ordered the doors closed and the lights put out.

"Now," his voice boomed in the darkness, "every man in the room must pass and rub his hands against the pot, and when the guilty man touches it, the cock will crow."

The men filed past the pot, feeling for it in the dark. They reached down and touched it as they passed. The rooster was silent.

"Light the candles," Dow ordered, and he looked around at the men surrounding him. Somebody cheated, Dow thundered, and he looked at all the hands.

All had soot marks — except one. Dow held up the soot-free hands, and pronounced him guilty.

They searched the man with the clean hands, and found the missing purse.

Another time, Dow was on the road and came to a house. He knocked on the door and asked the woman who came to the door if he could stay the night. No, she said, her husband wasn't home.

But she changed her mind, and soon Dow was asleep in a back room.

Then he heard noises. Another man — not her husband — had come in, and he heard them joking with each other.

Suddenly, the husband knocked on the door, just back from the grog shop, and the wife quickly hid her caller in a bundle of raw cotton at the foot of Dow's bed.

The husband was boisterous, and the wife shushed him, saying Lorenzo Dow was in the house.

"Lorenzo Dow, the man who raises the devil?" shouted the husband. "Where is he? I want to see him raise the devil."

Dow led the husband into the bedroom, where the trembling visitor hid in the pile of cotton.

"If you will stand in the door, and give him a few thumps as he passes, but not so hard as to break his bones, I will see if I can raise him," he told the husband.

Then he touched the candle to the bundle of cotton, which flamed up immediately, and the hidden man jumped up in a mass of living fire and broke for the door. The husband rapped "the devil" across the shoulders as he passed, and ever after marveled at the preacher who could "raise the devil."

No hardship was too much for Dow, if he thought he could save a soul in the wilderness. Writing in his journal, he said:

"We prepared our kettle of coffee, and partook with gratitude, and found we here could sing praises to God, not without a sense of the Divine favor, considering our situation a little before, we lay down to rest as under the wing of the Almighty in this desert, inhabited only by wild beasts, whilst the wolves were howling over every side."

There was one story — it may even be true — about Dow visiting Pickens County in 1819. It seems the ruffians chased him out of a settlement, and shouted after him:

"Hey, parson, we haven't named our town. What name would you suggest?"

Dow turned in his saddle with a scowl and shouted: "Reform! Reform!"

And that, so the story goes, is how Reform got its name.

Chapter Ten

1807 A. D.

Patriot or man without a country? Aaron Burr captured in Alabama

It was iron cold, the night of Feb. 18, 1807, and the two young men could hear the wolves howling outside in the Alabama wilderness.

They shivered, and one of them tossed another log on the fire. The sparks fluttered like a flock of bright wild geese, and they rose in the fireplace of the little cabin. The men turned back to their backgammon game.

The two were Nicholas Perkins, a lawyer and land agent, and Thomas Malone, a clerk of the court. The cabin was one in a cluster of buildings in the county seat of Wakefield, in Washington County, near Fort Stoddert and St. Stephens on the Tombigbee River.

Shortly after 10 p.m., they looked up each other. There was another sound out there, the tramp of horse's hoof beats, approaching the cabin. Perkins opened the door, and there were two men on horseback, the steam of the horses' breaths flaring white in the darkness.

Which way to Colonel John Hinson's house? one of the men wanted to know.

Perkins pointed the way, but warned it was seven miles away, and the creek was up from recent rains.

As they talked, the fire in the cabin flared up, and Perkins looked at the man who asked the questions. He was dressed like a river boatman, coarse pantaloons of homespun, a roundabout cloak of inferior drab cloth, and a dingy wide-brimmed beaver hat.

But, Perkins noticed, he rode a fine spirited horse, with an expensive saddle and new holsters for his pistols. And, beneath the homespun pantaloons, Perkins could see a pair of expensive boots.

Most of all, Perkins noticed his eyes. They sparkled like diamonds in the flickering firelight.

The travelers left, moving out of the circle of light and into the darkness, heading for Hinson's house, and Perkins turned to Malone.

"That's Aaron Burr," he breathed. "I have read a description of him in the proclamation. I cannot be mistaken. Let us follow him to Hinson's and take measures for his arrest."

Follow him? In the middle of the night? Malone shrugged, and shook his head.

But Perkins, convinced he had seen Burr, went to the home of Theodore Brightwell, the sheriff. The two of them swung onto their horses and headed through the woods toward the Hinson house.

The proclamation Perkins spoke of had come from Gov. Robert Williams of the Mississippi Territory (Alabama was then part of the Mississippi Territory) and it offered a $12,000 reward for information about Burr.

The proclamation, branding Burr a fugitive, was the low point in an illustrious career which had carried Burr to the vice presidency and within a single vote — in the House of Representatives — of being President of the United States.

He had fought in the American Revolution, rising from private to lieutenant colonel under Washington. He had served New York as a state legislator and was elected to the U.S. Senate in 1791.

Then he ran with Thomas Jefferson for the presidency, both in 1796 and 1800. Everyone knew Burr was really the Republican choice for vice president, but the way the original Constitution was worded, both men technically were running for the same office, the presidency.

Jefferson was elected vice president under John Adams in 1796, then he and Burr won the election in 1800, receiving the same number of votes for president.

Everyone expected Burr to step back out of contention and take the vice presidency, but he refused. The contest went to the U. S. House of Representatives, and for ballot after ballot, Jefferson and Burr tied for the top office.

Then Alexander Hamilton, Jefferson's old enemy, stepped into the picture. He hated Jefferson, but he distrusted Burr even more, and he threw his support in the House to Jefferson. On the 36th ballot, with Hamilton's help, Jefferson finally was elected President.

And Burr, with those hard sparkling eyes, looked at Hamilton with hatred — the man who had cost him the nation's highest office. Later, in 1804, while he was serving as vice president, Burr ran for governor of New York, and Hamilton beat him again.

The hatred overflowed into action, and Burr challenged Hamilton to a duel. On July 11, 1804, at Weehawken, N.J., Burr carefully took aim and killed Hamilton with one shot from a dueling pistol. A new Jersey grand jury indicted him for murder, and Burr fled back to Washington, presiding over the Senate—immune from arrest—until his term ended.

Out of office, Burr was ruined politically. He traveled to the west, visiting Henry Clay and Gen. Andrew Jackson. Some say he planned to lead a movement to break the western part of the U.S. away from the nation and set up a new country.

Others saw a plot for Burr to take over the Spanish territories and Mexico, and create a new nation there.

He was arrested in Kentucky and released. Then, with 13 riverboats and 60 armed men, he came down the Mississippi. He was met, a few miles above Natchez, by state troops sent by Gov. Robert Williams of Mississippi.

He was arrested, his boats and guns confiscated, and trial was scheduled. His friends got him out of jail on $10,000 bond.

On the morning of the trial, Burr didn't show up in court, and Williams issued a proclamation for his arrest.

Burr and a companion, Maj. Robert Ashley, fled eastward through the Mississippi wilds, into Alabama. And, on the night of Feb. 18, 1807, they reined their horses in at the cabin of Nicholas Perkins.

They asked for Hinson's place because Hinson had been in Natchez, and had told Burr to come and stay with him if he came to Alabama.

Now, in the bitter cold night, Perkins and Sheriff

Brightwell forded the muddy creek, and moved on through the dark pines to Hinson's cabin.

Burr and Ashley had arrived. Hinson was away from home, and Mrs. Hinson fixed supper for the two.

At one point, while Burr was out of the room, Mrs. Hinson (she had talked with the sheriff, who was her relative) turned to Ashley and said:

"Have I not, sir, the honor of entertaining Colonel Burr, the gentleman who has just walked out?"

Ashley walked out of the room, giving her no answer. Meanwhile, Perkins was dismayed that Brightwell did not arrest Burr on the spot. He rode through the night to nearby Fort Stoddert on the Tombigbee and told Capt. Edward P. Gaines his story.

Gaines led a file of mounted soldiers back toward Hinson's house, and met Burr and Ashley near a ferry on the Tombigbee. Burr was on his way to Pensacola and safety with the Spaniards.

The riders pulled up when they saw the soldiers, and Gaines reined in his horse.

"I presume, sir, I have the honor of addressing Colonel Burr," he said.

Burr's eyes glinted.

"I am a traveler in the country, and do not recognize your right to ask such a question," he told the captain.

"I arrest you on the instance of the federal government," said Gaines.

Burr's eyes flashed again, and he looked down his patrician nose at the upstart captain. "You are a young man, and may not be aware of the responsibilities which result from arresting travelers."

Gaines stared him down. "My mind is made up. You must accompany me to Fort Stoddert, where you will be treated with all the respect due the ex-vice president of the United States, so long as you make no attempt to escape from me."

Burr wheeled his horse around, and rode with Gaines and the soldiers back toward the fort.

(It is a mystery why Sheriff Brightwell did not arrest Burr. It is assumed by historians that Burr talked him into helping him to escape.)

Later, Nicholas Perkins commanded the soldiers who took Burr up through Alabama, through Georgia and up the East Coast to his trial at Richmond.

On the journey, Burr slept in a tent while Perkins (Malone went along on the trip too) and his men slept outside on the ground.

They crossed the Chattahoochee in canoes, with the horses swimming alongside. Perkins let Burr carry two pistols for his protection against possible Indian attacks.

At Chester, S. C., Burr jumped from his horse and shouted to a crowd of men: "I am Aaron Burr, under military arrest, and claim the protection of the civil authorities."

Perkins, knowing that Burr had much support in South Carolina, pulled his pistols and ordered Burr to get back onto his horse.

"I will not," said Burr, firmly standing his ground.

Perkins threw down his pistols, grabbed Burr around the waist and threw him back onto his horse. Malone seized the reins of Burr's horse, and the soldiers whipped the horse into action. Soon they were outside the range of the civilians.

On the outskirts of the town, Burr burst into a flood of tears and Malone, recognizing a great man brought low, cried with him.

Later, in Richmond, Burr was brought to trial for treason, charged with conspiring to take over part of the western United States and make a separate country.

President Jefferson sent him wine and food in jail, but pushed for conviction. Chief Justice John Marshall of the U.S. Supreme Court presided over the trial, and interpreted such a narrow view of treason that Burr was acquitted.

After his trial, Burr went to Europe and tried to revive his scheme of a separate country from the Spanish possessions, but he couldn't bring it off.

In 1812, he returned to the U.S. under an assumed name, Adolphus Arnot. In time, he practiced law in New York, under his own name again.

He died in 1836. On his deathbed, he disavowed any treason toward the United States.

Burr's life illuminates the kind of phenomenon which occasionally bursts across the sky of American politics — a charming man, a charismatic personality with great leadership ability, but with one fatal flaw: overvaulting ambition.

Burr could have gone down in history as a great American leader, but instead is viewed as a traitor, a man without a country. As always, with men such as Burr, it is fascinating to consider what might have been.

Chapter Eleven

1807 A. D.

'We may perish... But we shall not slumber': Alabama's Declaration of Independence

The rider galloped into the pine clearing, waving a piece of paper. People came out of the log cabins to gather around the rider, who had pushed his panting horse hard for the 75 miles up from Mobile.

One man took the piece of paper and climbed onto a stump to read it. More people streamed into the clearing — men with axes, women pulling children behind them.

It was early in September of 1807 in the town of Wakefield on the Tombigbee River. The county — now Washington County — was then part of the Mississippi Territory.

The man read from the paper, and there were curses from the crowd. The captain of the British warship *Leopard* had stopped a U.S. frigate, the *Chesapeake*, and demanded to search the American vessel.

The American captain had angrily refused, and the British ship fired on the *Chesapeake*. Then the British marines dragged off four sailors, calling them deserters from the British navy. One of the American sailors was hanged from the yardarm of the British ship.

The incident happened in June 1807. The American ship sailed back home, and the captain told his story. Now, in September, the word was just filtering through to the Alabama-Mississippi frontier.

The meeting in the clearing broke up. The women and children went back to the log cabins, and some of the men gathered in the tavern, a low building built of logs. Tankards of ale were raised, and fists pounded on the bar.

How dare the British board our ship? Who the hell do they think they are, rulers of the world? By God, we ought to go to war with them again, if that's what it takes for us to be free!

The men in the tavern had troubles. They were stuck off in the Alabama woods, surrounded by Indians. The Spanish, who held Mobile to the south, charged the American settlers a 12 percent tax on the goods coming in or going out of the port. And the men felt that the rest of the United States, people in the eastern seaboard states, didn't care about them.

"Let's send a message to Congress," one man said, "and tell them how we feel."

"Won't do no good," another said.

"Let's send it anyway," another insisted, and a meeting was set.

On Sept. 8, 1807, in the big log cabin they called a courthouse, the men gathered. Standing at the end of the room at the judge's bench was Col. James Caller, who presided.

Colonel Caller was the man Aaron Burr wanted to see back in February of that year about Burr's ill-fated scheme to take over the American West. But Caller, a patriot, wouldn't see him.

"We think and feel on the occasion as every American thinks and feels," they wrote. "We despise the bully and the coward who, as captain of the *Leopard*, was the instrument of exhibiting the enormous extent of the claims of the pretended Mistress of the Ocean."

The colonel raised his hand as he read on.

"Is national independence a dream? Shall Great Britain or any other nation come at pleasure into territory and lay hold of whomsoever she pleases under the pretense that this is her subject and that man is in her employ—that there is a felon, and there a deserter?

"Our national ships are our territory, in whatever quarter of the world they are found ... We care not who the men were that were demanded from the *Chesapeake*; we care not whence they came, where they were born, nor who claimed allegiance from them."

Cheers broke out from the other men in the room, and Caller held up his hand again.

"England may count upon our divisions. She is mistaken. The violence of her conduct has united all America. Our own settlement originally consists, and still in a great degree consists, of those who adhered to England in the Revolutionary War.

"Old factions are forgotten; we all view with the same sensibility any outrage on the honor of our common country; and old Whigs and old Tories will cordially unite in devoting their lives and fortunes to avenge the wounded dignity of America against the insults and oppressions of any government upon earth."

The document made no bones about it — the men from Washington County were calling for war with England.

"War will indeed open a new theatre for the talents of our rule; but we have a strong confidence that the intellectual and moral preeminence which, amidst the convulsions of the world, has been so conspicuous in peace, will not become extinct on the instant of the appearance of war.

"As to ourselves and our local concerns, it is true we have sometimes feared that we were overlooked in the council of the nation. Our population is small; we are surrounded, except on the Spanish side, by the most powerful tribes of Indians existing within the original limits of the United States.

"Yet, few as we are, we consider ourselves as an advanced guard, destined to defend the immense tract of valuable territory which lies between the settlements on the Mobile (River) and the state of Tennessee.

"We may perish at our posts, but we shall not slumber there."

Then the document listed, like a string of prayer beads, the complaints against the Spanish in Mobile.

They had to pay the 12 percent tax, whether coming into port or going out.

"We continue to pay a double price for the commodities of Europe; we will again, if need be, pay sixteen dollars per barrel for the flour of Kentucky, whilst our neighbors at the Natchez, unencumbered by the Spanish obstacles, are paying only four; we will view these things light as compared with a deliberate, and authorized, and systematic violation of our territory by a foreign power."

Caller now raised his voice into a shout, he was

coming to the end.

"We will devote ourselves to our country at large, and from this moment cease to seek any other object than permanence to national existence and reality to national independence.

"The charter of that independence was drawn up in '76; it was ratified by the peace of '83; but it still cries out for the blood of American citizens to seal it and to give it practical validity. Our blood shall be mingled with that of other Americans in offering the solemn sacrifice."

There were cheers, and the men in the log courthouse adopted the document, unanimously. It was voted to send a copy of the declaration to the President of the United States, and it was duly signed by the chairman, Colonel Caller.

The next day, a rider folded the paper into his saddlebag and clopped through the pine trees toward Mobile and the next ship for the east coast.

The declaration by the Alabamians was received by Congress and went straight into a pigeonhole. But almost five years later, the call for war against Great Britain, from a group of log cabin pioneers in Alabama, was answered.

On June 1, 1812, President James Madison asked the U.S. Congress to declare war on Great Britain. The war of 1812 — some called it the second war for American independence — began when Congress declared war on June 18, 1812.

+++++++++++

(Note: The declaration from Alabama first appeared in state papers in 1834, and then passed into obscurity for 91 years. The only known copy of the original turned up in a New York auction room and was bought by the Huntington Library of California, which gave permission to republish it.

The declaration may have been the first piece of printing — at least one of the first — in Alabama. On the last page of the declaration, an unknown printer apologized for his printing job.

"Printed on the Mobile," it said. "The printer apologizes for the execution of his work; his types are old and much worn, and the situation of the country does not justify his purchasing new ones."

*"...Few as we are, we consider
ourselves as an advanced guard,
destined to defend the immense
tract of valuable territory which
lies between the settlements on
the Mobile (River) and the state
of Tennessee."*

Chapter Twelve

1811 A. D.

'Let the white race perish!' he shouted: Tecumseh warns the Creeks of the coming flood

The flocks of wild ducks arrowed toward the south. Chestnuts hung ripe in the forest. And there was a chill of the coming winter, that October day of 1811.

The Indian warriors, dressed in finery, came first in hundreds, then in thousands to the old Creek town of Tuckabatche, on the Tallapoosa River.

A white man, Big Sam Dale, hid in an empty lodge and looked out on the square of the town. He watched the warriors, five thousand of them, gather in the square, leaving an open space in the middle. There was the musical murmur of talk, then there was quiet.

A slim, muscular Indian, dressed only in a breech-cloth and with two crane feathers in his hair, strode through the Creek warriors. He carried a war club, painted red, and his jaw was set straight ahead.

Behind him came his bodyguards, more than a dozen Shawnee dressed as he was, carrying their war clubs and looking straight ahead.

The slim young chief circled the flag pole three times and emptied his pouch of tobacco and sumac onto a fire at the base of the pole.

Then, arching above the crowd, came the un-earthly sound of the Shawnee war whoop, sounded by the young chief, and the Shawnee dancers flung them-selves into a war dance.

It was all there, in the dance of the shining red bodies: the ambush, the stalking of the enemy, the smash of the attack, the enemy killed, then the swift flash of the scalping knife and the hand thrust high with the symbol of victory.

The sweating dancers moved back, leaving the young chief standing alone in the midst of the great crowd. Again, there was silence.

It was Tecumseh, great chief of the Shawnee, come down to Alabama from Ohio on his great crusade for Indian unity.

The young Indian leader had seen the old Indian chiefs, greedy for the white man's baubles and gold, sell out Indian territory and bask rich on the land while their tribes went hungry.

Tecumseh saw, saw clearly, that the stream of white people coming through the gaps in the Appala-chians would not cease. The white flood would con-tinue, into Ohio, into Kentucky, into Alabama and

Tennessee and Mississippi—unless they were stopped. His cause was the oldest in human history, to be free. His answer: Stop the white people, by whatever means, stop them now, and save the lands of the Indians.

To do this, to stem the white flood, Tecumseh was trying to gather all the Indian tribes against the common enemy. He was trying to weld all the Indian tribes together, from the Canadian border to the Gulf of Mexico, to unite them in war against the white invaders.

His crusade was riding on this speech, that day in October at Tuckabatche on the Tallapoosa. He had failed in Mississippi, had put his soaring oratory before the Choctaws, only to be defused by the Choctaw chief Pushmataha.

Pushmataha spoke in soothing tones. He spoke of cooperating with the whites. They would be fair. They would allow the Indians to hold onto their lands. They would abide by their treaties. Tecumseh had listened. Then he shook his head and left. The Choctaws would not join him.

Now, with the Creeks, it was all or nothing. If he failed, his crusade would die aborning. If he won over the Creeks, he would have a fighting chance.

Big Sam Dale looked out the window of the Indian lodge and listened, as Tecumseh spoke to the great gathering. The chief's voice rose over the crowd:

"Accursed be the race that has seized on our country and made women of our warriors! Our fathers from their graves reproach us as slaves and cowards. I hear them now in the wailing winds."

Some of the listening warriors nodded their heads, and raised their tomahawks in agreement.

"Oh Muscogee, brothers of my mother, brush from your eyes the sleep of slavery! Once more strike for vengeance—once more for your country! The spirits of the mighty dead complain. Their tears drop from the weeping skies.

"Let the white race perish! They seize your land, they corrupt your women, they trample on the grass of your dead. Back whence they came, upon a trail of blood, they must be driven. Back, back, aye, into the great waters whose accursed waves brought them to our shores.

"Burn their houses, destroy their stock! The red man owns the country and the palefaces must never enjoy it. War now, war forever!

"Kill the old chiefs, friends of peace. Kill the cattle, the hogs and fowls. Destroy the wheels and looms. Throw away the plows and everything used by the Americans. Shake your war clubs, shake yourselves, and you will frighten the Americans. The arms will drop from their hands. The ground will become a bog and mire them, and you may knock them on the head with your war clubs."

By now, Tecumseh's voice had risen to fever pitch with the intensity of his hatred. The Creek warriors, swept along by his oratory, shouted in agreement. Among the Creeks was the half blood William Weatherford, Red Eagle to the Indians, later to lead the Creeks in their war against the whites.

Big Sam Dale, watching from his hiding place, wrote later:

"His eyes burned with supernatural lustre, and his whole frame trembled with emotion: his voice resounded over the multitude — now sinking in low and musical whispers, now rising to its highest key, hurling out his words like a succession of thunderbolts."

Even in the face of his soaring words, the Creek chiefs held out. Big Warrior, a huge bulk of a half blood and a chief of the Creeks, told the gathering that Tecumseh was a "bad man."

Tecumseh pointed his finger at Big Warrior.

"Your blood is white. You have taken my talk, and

the sticks (a bundle of red sticks, signifying war), and the wampum, and the hatchet, but you do not mean to fight. I know the reasons. You do not believe the Great Spirit has sent me. You shall know! When I return to the Tippecanoe (a river in Indiana), I shall stamp my foot and the very earth will tremble."

Tecumseh and his bodyguards left immediately for Georgia, to try and enlist the Cherokees in their cause.

Beginning on the night of Dec. 16, 1811, at a time when the Creeks had calculated that Tecumseh was back in Indiana, on the Tippecanoe River, a series of great earthquakes struck the Mississippi Valley, and rumbles were heard in Alabama.

The Creeks were shaken, they were impressed by the stamping of Tecumseh's foot. Weatherford found it easier to recruit soldiers for his war party, and the Indian wars soon broke out in earnest — Creeks resisting the white men in force.

In the north, Tecumseh fought. He was commissioned a brigadier in the British Army and led his Indians troops in a battle against the Americans on the Thames River in Canada, near Detroit, Mich.

Kentucky riflemen killed him in the battle. It is said they scalped him, flayed his body, and distributed strips of his skin for razor strops. He was 44 years old.

Pushmataha, by resisting Tecumseh and holding his Choctaws in line, became a favorite of the whites. When he died, he was buried with military honors in Washington, D.C. and his funeral cortege was more than a mile long. His body now lies under an impressive monument in the Congressional cemetery near the capitol.

Tecumseh, the champion of the Indians, the man who saw what was happening and gave his life to fight it, lies in an unmarked grave on the banks of the Thames River in Canada.

Chapter Thirteen

1812 A. D.

Gen. James Wilkinson Takes Mobile from the Spanish: Patriot? Spy? Traitor? Double Agent? Hero?

A smile crept across the American general's face as he unfolded the orders from Washington.

The general, James Wilkinson, sat in his office in the Cabildo at New Orleans and looked out across the Mississippi, to the east, toward Mobile.

The smile grew broader. Wilkinson had been a

double agent — a career American Army officer, but the Spanish had been slipping him money steadily over the years. At one time, he admitted taking $17,000 from Spain.

He exposed Aaron Burr's plans to create another country in the American West, and some thought he did this to divert attention from his own role as a foreign agent.

Wilkinson was slippery. He was court-martialed, but acquitted, in February 1812. He was given what one writer called a "spotted coat of white wash."

The War of 1812 began in June of 1812, with the new country of America fighting Britain a second time. The war put Wilkinson in the saddle again, as commanding officer of the American forces at New Orleans.

Now, he looked at the piece of paper again, the orders from Washington: Take Mobile and West Florida from the Spanish.

Imagine a thin slice of the Gulf Coast stretching from the Mississippi River to the Georgia line — the Chattahoochee River.

Imagine this slice cut into three pieces — from the Mississippi River in Louisiana east to the Pearl River in Mississippi, from the Pearl east to the Perdido, just west of Pensacola, and from the Perdido to the Chattahoochee, the Georgia line.

All three slices of territory stretched only a few miles north of the Gulf Coast, the northern boundary of Spanish West Florida running along 31 degrees north.

This meant the Spanish owned Mobile and the part of Alabama from Mobile up to Mount Vernon. It also meant the Spanish controlled the port, and thus held a firm grip on the river system of Alabama.

The Alabamians who lived above the line had to pay a heavy duty on goods passing through Spanish Mobile. Settlers on the Mississippi paid $4 for a sack of Kentucky flour, while the Spanish tax boosted the price in Alabama to $16.

The Alabamians pleaded with U.S. authorities to annex the small strip of territory — to take over Mobile — but President James Madison was watching the European situation, and he was cautious.

The settlers who lived in the Louisiana and Mississippi got tired of waiting. On Sept. 26, 1810, they held a convention and declared their independence. And if the U.S. didn't want them, well, they would set up their own country, by God.

They issued their "Declaration of Independence," which said, in part:

"Being thus left without any hope of protection from the mother country (the U.S.) and exposed to all the evils of a state of anarchy ... it becomes our duty to provide for our own security, as a free and independent state, absolved from all allegiance to a government which no longer protects us."

The rebels were a feisty group. Along with declaring their independence they declared war on the Spanish in Mobile, and even sent an army to take the city. Their raid was ineffective.

But the idea worked. President Madison read their declaration and got busy. He issued a proclamation declaring the new nation to be part of the U.S., saying it was part of the Louisiana Purchase bought from France in 1803.

On Dec. 6, 1812, Americans from New Orleans reached St. Francisville, La., and raised the flag of the U.S. There was no opposition; this was what most of the settlers wanted anyway. Even now, these are called the "Florida parishes" of Louisiana.

That same December, President Madison piloted a resolution through Congress. On Jan. 10, Congress authorized Madison to occupy Mobile and the part of West Florida from the Pearl River to the Perdido.

John Armstrong, the new secretary of war, forwarded the orders to the American commander in New

Orleans — the same James Wilkinson who had admitted taking $17,000 from the Spanish.

The wily Wilkinson had advised his government to take Mobile. On March 4, 1813, Wilkinson began preparations for invasion.

In April, he landed below Mobile with 600 men; he knew there were only 60 Spaniards in Fort Charlotte. He placed his cannon above the town, and anchored his gunboats off the city in the bay.

On April 12, Wilkinson sent a polite note to Cayetano Perez, the Spanish commandant in Fort Charlotte:

"The troops of the United States under my command do not approach as enemies of Spain, but by order of the President they come to relieve the garrison which you command from the occupancy of a post within the legitimate limits of these (United) States.

"I therefore hope, sir, that you may peacefully retire from Fort Charlotte, and from the bounds of the Mississippi Territory (and proceed) east of the Perdido River with the garrison you command."

Perez protested, but he looked at his few men, then he looked over the walls of Fort Charlotte at the dug-in Americans. He looked at the cannon north of the fort, and the gunboats anchored in the bay, and he ran up the white flag.

At 5 p.m. on April 13, with salutes booming out from the cannon on shore and smoke puffing out from the gunboats, the American flag was unfurled above Fort Charlotte.

And so, after more than 100 years of rule by the French, the British and the Spanish, Mobile and the tip of Alabama became truly American.

The other slice of the West Florida pie — the slice from the Perdido River to the Chattahoochee, from Pensacola to the Georgia line — was bought by the U.S. in 1819, from Spain.

"The Alabamians pleaded with U.S. authorities to...take over Mobile-but President James Madison was watching the European situation, and he was cautious."

Chapter Fourteen

1813 A. D.

The Creek Red Sticks attacked at noon and 500 died in Fort Mims Massacre

The pioneer Alabama woman heard a noise at the front door of her cabin and wheeled around quickly, her sage broom raised as a weapon.

But it was only an Indian boy, crying as he shivered in his shabby buckskins.

The woman put down her broom and led the orphan inside, drying his tears with the hem of her skirt. She gave him a bowl of soup from the big black pot.

When the soup was gone, the boy looked up at her, tears still streaking his cheeks, and smiled. The woman smiled back.

Later the woman — a half blood Creek who had married a white man — talked with her husband. They couldn't just throw him back into the woods to die. Yes, they agreed, they would adopt him as a son, and raise him.

The Indian boy grew to young manhood in the white family, working in the fields and romping in the woods with the other children. Then he felt a yearning for Indian life, and left the sorrowing family to join his Creek tribe.

It was now August of 1813 and the white couple — Zachariah and Vicey McGirth — had brought their eight children to Fort Mims in South Alabama for protection.

A band of Creeks were bringing guns and ammunition to the north from Pensacola when a group of whites attacked them. It was the Battle of Burnt Corn, and the war was on.

The Creeks, having scattered the band of whites, felt they could defeat any white army, and gathered a huge war party.

Leading the warlike "Red Sticks" was William Weatherford, the half blood called Red Eagle by the Creeks. Other Creeks leaders were Peter McQueen, Far-Off Warrior, High-Head Jim, and a host of prophets.

The whites in the vicinity of Lake Tensaw, in Baldwin County, had gathered in a stockade around the home of Samuel Mims. The inside of the stockade was packed with tents, which the white families had thrown up, and small children scampered about amid the confusion.

About 175 soldiers had been sent to Fort Mims to protect the settlers, and there were about 550 people jammed inside the stockade, including 100 children.

Major Daniel Beasley commanded the soldiers. He felt there was little chance of an Indian attack.

Two black slaves, sent out to watch some cattle grazing nearby, came rushing back to the fort, their eyes wide with alarm. Indians! they said; Indians in war paint! They had seen them in the woods!

Beasley listened, and tried to calm the fears of the settlers.

He sent out some horsemen to investigate, but they found nothing; no sign of a war party.

One of the blacks was beaten, for unduly alarming the settlers. A fabrication, scoffed Beasley.

It was noon on Aug. 30, 1813, and a drum roll was heard from inside the fort, summoning the soldiers to the noon meal. As the soldiers filed inside the eastern gate of the fort, nobody noticed that recent rains had washed up a small embankment of sand against the gate.

Four hundred yards to the east, a thousand Creek warriors lay in wait, hidden by a ravine. When the drum roll was heard, they rose to their feet and charged across the open space, yelling and waving war clubs and rifles.

Beasley saw them coming, and tried to close the eastern gate. But the piled-up sand jammed it, and it would not swing shut. The onrushing Indians knocked him to the ground and killed him, and swept into the fort.

Inside, there was bedlam. Indian warriors bashed the heads of soldiers and women and children alike. Scalps were ripped from their heads, and slung onto Indian belts. There was a frenzy of killing and scalping. The British had offered $5 a scalp.

One of the frenzied warriors was Sanota, the orphan Indian boy who had been befriended by Zachariah and Vicey McGirth many years before.

And, huddled in the corner of one of the buildings

inside the stockade, trying to calm her children, was Vicey McGirth.

The plundering Indians broke into the buildings inside the stockade, killing and scalping the people inside.

The door of one building burst open, and Sanota — who had been busy hacking women and children to death — saw his foster mother and her children in the corner of the cabin.

A flash of recognition, and the bloodthirsty Sanota became a kind-hearted protector. He stood before Mrs. McGirth and her children and warded off the other Indians. These are my slaves, he proclaimed, leave them alone.

And, as Mrs. McGirth and her children watched in horror, the Indians butchered the other white people in the cabin.

When it was over, blood stood in puddles inside the stockade. A total of 517 people — soldiers, women, children, slaves — lay dead on the ground, scalps stripped from their heads.

It was one of the bloodiest massacres in American history, and out of it was born the battle cry: *Remember Fort Mims!* which spurred the whites to battle.

Word of bloody Fort Mims reached Andrew Jackson in Nashville, where he lay in his bed with a bullet wound in his arm, the result of a duel. Jackson knew that the Indians would have to be stopped now, or the whole Alabama frontier would be on fire.

"The health of your general is restored; he will command in person," said the ailing Jackson, and he led a volunteer army into Alabama to fight the Creeks.

On March 27, 1814, Jackson and his army surrounded the Creeks at a place called Horseshoe Bend on the Tallapoosa River.

The Indians were defeated, and their power broken. Jackson became a national hero.

From Horseshoe Bend, it was only a moment in

time until the Creeks were walking the Trail of Tears to exile in Oklahoma, leaving their rich lands to the flood of incoming white settlers.

After the battle of Fort Mims, Sanota — the Creek brave raised by the white family — took Mrs. McGirth and her children north with him toward his home on the Tallapoosa, calling them his slaves and protecting them from other Creeks.

One day he told Mrs. McGirth he was going to fight Jackson at the Horseshoe, and she must try to get away to the south if he was killed.

Sanota was killed by the Americans at Horseshoe Bend, and Mrs. McGirth headed southward, trying to find her husband, who had been away from the fort on the day of the massacre.

At Mobile, Zachariah McGirth — who had given up his family for dead — was told that some people wanted to see him down at the wharf. He went down to the river, and saw a group of shabby Indians, waiting.

He walked closer, peering at them, then uttered a cry of joy. His wife and children ran forward to embrace him, and the McGirths were together again.

Chapter Fifteen

1813 A. D.

Frightened settlers and dogs of war beat back Creek attackers

In the steaming August heat of 1813, Fort Sinquefield stank of too many people, too many dogs and not enough air.

Rumors of an Indian uprising had swept across the countryside, after an inconclusive battle at Burnt Corn. Settlers in the fork of the Alabama and Tombigbee rivers had gathered in the rude log fortress called Fort Sinquefield.

A three-foot trench had been dug, in which 15-foot pine trees stood to form a barricade. Inside the square stockade stood a two-story blockhouse, which looked out over the level of the outside walls.

Behind the barricade, families of settlers gathered around their tents. There were crying children, a pack of barking hound dogs, and a number of worried parents, peeping between the logs.

The husbands, looking down their rifle barrels at the brush close by the fort, wondered if their homes and barns nearby would be burned.

Now, with the heat and the stink of the crowded stockade in their nostrils, two families — those of Abner James and Ransom Kimbell — talked it over.

There had been no Indian attacks, there seemed to be no danger, the children were unhappy about having to stay in the tiny half acre enclosure ... why not go back to their nearby homes?

The decision was made. The two families packed their sleeping gear. The tents were struck. The men hefted their rifles to their shoulders, the happy children whistled for the dogs, and the log gate creaked open to let them out.

They did not know that on Sept. 1, 1813, the Creeks had gone on the warpath. The "Red Sticks," the warlovers of the Creek Nation, had been stirred up by Tecumseh, the great Shawnee chief. He had come south from Michigan to urge the Creeks, the Choctaws, the Chickasaws, the Cherokees, to fight the white man to the death, or lose all the Indian lands.

The day before — on Aug. 30, 1813 — the "Red Sticks,'" led by Red Eagle, the half blood William Weatherford, had swooped down on Fort Mims and killed all but a handful of the 500 people inside.

The war was on, but the word had not reached Fort Sinquefield.

In mid-August, the Creeks had collected at the Holy Ground, a gathering place on the Alabama River, and formed two divisions, one to attack Fort Mims, the other to overpower the white people at Fort Sinquefield.

Now, an Indian prophet named Josiah Francis led a party of about 125 warriors toward Sinquefield. About 3 p.m. on Sept. 1, Francis and his warriors surrounded the Kimbell house near Bassett's Creek.

Isham Kimbell, 16 years old, heard the whooping and came out of the blacksmith shop — about 150 yards from the main house — and saw the Indians begin their bloody work, killing and scalping his family.

Young Kimbell grabbed his little brother and started running for nearby Fort Sinquefield. A band of Indians chased them through the woods, firing as they ran, the musket balls cutting the chinquapin bushes around them.

On crossing a stream, Isham fell. When he got up, his little brother was gone, and was never seen again. Isham stumbled on toward the fort, and finally made it behind the log walls.

Other members of his family and the James family filtered into the fort, having escaped the massacre at the Kimbell home.

Night came on, and a gentle rain began to fall. A body stirred in the pile of corpses outside the Kimbell house, and a woman — stripped of her hair and scalp by an Indian knife — struggled to her feet.

Desperately, she moved bodies aside, crying as she worked to find her small son. She found her one-year-old baby, and its body was still warm. She nursed the baby and the warm nourishment revived the infant.

Now, with the baby in her arms, blood streaming down her face, Mrs. Sarah Merrill — the daughter of Abner James — stumbled through the woods toward the nearby fort.

Toward daylight, the riflemen peering through the logs saw the apparition approaching the fort — a woman without hair or scalp, head bloody, plodding toward safety. They ran out of the fort and helped her inside.

Back there, she gasped, back there she had left her baby in a hollow log because she could not carry it farther. One of the brave men slipped into the early dawn, found the log, found the baby, and brought him back to the fort.

Next morning, Sept. 3, a contingent of American soldiers — some say seven soldiers and three scouts, others say 19 soldiers — came from nearby Fort Madison to help with the terrible task of burying the bodies from the Kimbell-James massacre.

The bodies were brought by ox cart from the Kimbell house to a spot near the fort, and nearly everyone in the fort came outside to bow their heads for the mass funeral. An old man named Phillips, sitting beside the gateway, saw some wild turkeys advancing through the low brush. He rubbed his eyes, yes, they were turkeys.

But Isham Kimbell, the 16-year-old boy who had escaped the massacre, had sharper eyes. He looked, looked again, and yelled. The turkeys were Indians, creeping, bent over at the waist, through the brush.

There was a stampede for the gate of the fort, men grabbed children, women raised their skirts and ran, and they made it inside — just before the gate slammed shut in the faces of the charging warriors.

But everyone didn't make it. There were about 10 women at the spring just outside the fort. They were cut off, and the Indians turned toward them.

Suddenly a hero sprang up, large as life, on the scene. Isaac Hayden (called Heaton by Pickett in *"History of Alabama"*) sat on his horse inside the fort.

Hayden was either just back from a deer hunt, accompanied by a large pack of hounds (says Pickett) or he was a soldier in the burial party (according to a book about Clarke County by a Rev. T. H. Ball).

There were close to 60 yapping hound dogs inside

the fort, sniffing through the logs, jumping on the wall, trying to get outside.

Hayden opened the gate of the fort, and sicked the dogs on the Indians. Then he galloped his horse toward the trapped women, urging his dogs onward.

The startled Creek warriors were forced to halt and defend themselves from the fury of the "dogs of war." While the Indians were fighting off the dogs, Hayden helped the women run from the spring to the fort.

All but one made it to safety. A Mrs. Phillips, heavy with an unborn child, was caught by the warriors and scalped.

Then the furious Indians attacked the fort, losing many braves in the bloody frontal attack. But the white men fought them, and the Indians retired, taking the horses of the soldiers with them.

Thirty-five white men had fought off 100 Indians.

Next day, the settlers in Fort Sinquefield, knowing the Indians would return with reinforcements, left the small fort for the larger Fort Madison, in the fork of the two rivers.

After the Fort Mims massacre and the attack on Fort Sinquefield, the American settlers across the Southeast were alarmed. They went to Tennessee for help and Andrew Jackson came, leading an army which destroyed the power of the Creeks at Horseshoe Bend on the Tallapoosa River in March of 1814.

Twenty years later, the Creeks walked the road of exile, moving from Georgia and Alabama to Oklahoma along the "Trail of Tears."

In all the years of the Creek War, there probably were no more surprised Indians than the men of Prophet Francis, when the pack of yowling, biting, snarling hound dogs fell on them in the brush outside Fort Sinquefield.

Chapter Sixteen

1813 A. D.

An Alabama legend on the frontier: Big Sam in the Great Canoe Fight

Big Sam was in trouble.

He stood at the edge of the muddy river, just below the sandy bluff overlooking the Alabama River near Randon's Creek in Monroe County, and he saw most of his militiamen on the other side of the river.

Behind him, beyond the white bluff in the pine woods, the Indians were gathering for a rush on the little group of white men gathered at the river's edge.

Big Sam — Capt. Sam Dale, Indian scout — knew
the rush would come soon, and he knew that he and the
other white men would be lucky to keep their hair.

There was one small dugout canoe, not nearly big
enough to take them across the river.

The 41-year-old Dale, who stood six two and
weighed 190 pounds, looked around for a way out of the
trap. But there was no way. Indians at their rear, a
treacherous river at their front, and no way out.

Suddenly, a large Indian war canoe rounded a
bend in the river and headed toward the white men.
The Indians were naked and painted with bright war
paint, slashes of orange and white on their faces. A
panther skin encircled the head of the chief, who sat in
the bow of the canoe.

Dale ordered his men to open fire, and the boom of
muskets broke the stillness of the river. But the Indians crouched down in the canoe, with only their heads
and their muskets showing, and they returned the fire.

Big Sam saw his way out. Two of the Indians
jumped out of the canoe and made it to shore. Dale
called for volunteers to go out in their small canoe and
take the big Indian war canoe away from the warriors.

It would be their ticket across the river, the key to
unlock the trap.

A black man named Caesar took the paddle, and
Dale climbed into the dugout with James Smith, 25,
and Jeremiah Austill, 19.

Caesar pushed off from shore, and paddled the
small dugout toward the large Indian canoe, with nine
warriors waiting inside.

About 20 yards away, the three white men rose up
in the boat and gave the Indians a broadside from their
rifles. Unfortunately, the powder was wet, and only
one rifle went off.

Ten feet away, the chief recognized Dale, and gave
a whoop.

The youth lashed out at him with an oar, which

the chief dodged, and the Indian brought his gun down on Austill's head, just as the canoes came together.

At that moment, Dale and Smith rose up and smashed down with their rifles. Dale hit one Indian, and the gun was broken near the lock. Dale clutched at the barrel, and kept on fighting.

The black man, Caesar, had been ordered to hold the two canoes together, a human grappling hook. He grabbed the gunwales of the Indian canoe, and held on, as the white men slugged and clubbed above him.

In the middle of the muddy river, the two canoes swayed and bobbed with the thrashing bodies. Dale and Smith stood with one foot in one canoe and one foot in the other, and flailed about them with their clubs.

A warrior smashed his war club into Austill. Another warrior raised a club to dash out Austill's brains. Dale smashed his gun barrel across the Indian's head, and he slumped into the big canoe.

Austill shook his head, and recovered, and he knocked an Indian into the river with the club he had taken from him.

Dale's militiamen — who had gotten across the river safely — watched the fight from the opposite bank. There were cheers when the warrior splashed into the river.

Finally, it was over. Smith and Austill and Dale stood over eight bodies in the war canoe. Caesar stood with them, triumphant. They rowed to shore, and flung the bodies into the river, to the cheers of the militiamen.

It was revenge, for the Fort Mims massacre back in August of 1813, when more than 500 white people had been killed.

The day was Nov. 12, 1813, in the midst of the Indian wars in Alabama. The Creeks would be destroyed five months later, in March 1814, at Horseshoe Bend on the Tallapoosa River.

The canoe fight caught the imagination of the

public, and made Dale, Smith, Austill and Caesar into frontier heroes.

Dale was born in Virginia, and moved with his family to Georgia, where he grew up on the frontier. He became a trader, buying goods in Savannah, packing them into the Creek nation, and exchanging them for cattle and ponies from the Indians.

Dale was at Tukabatche — hiding in an Indian lodge as 5,000 warriors met outside — when the great Shawnee chief, Tecumseh, made his stirring speech to the Creeks, urging them to fight to the death against the whites.

A biographer tells another story about Dale's fighting ability.

"Some years before (the canoe fight), he was attacked by two warriors, who shouted their war whoop as he was kneeling down to drink and rushed upon him with their tomahawks.

"He knifed them both, and, though bleeding from five wounds, he retraced their trail nine miles, crept stealthily to their camp, brained three sleeping warriors and cut the thongs of a female prisoner who lay by their side.

"While in this act, however, a fourth (warrior) sprang upon him from behind a log. Taken at such a disadvantage and exhausted by the loss of blood, he sank under the serpent grasp of the savage, who, with a yell of triumph, drew his knife and in a few moments would have closed the contest.

"At that instant, however, the woman drove a tomahawk deep into the head of the Indian, and thus preserved the life of her deliverer."

After the Indian wars ended, Dale settled in Mississippi, and was elected to the legislature.

Once, according to his biographer, General Dale (Big Sam was now a general) was in Mobile and was hauled into court as an endorser on a note. The debt was in the hands of a stranger.

The aging Dale, up against it financially and unable to pay the note, sought out the creditor. He found him in the bar of a Mobile hotel.

"Sir," said the old general to the loan shark, "I have no money to pay this debt. The principal has property — make him pay it, or let me go home and work it out."

The loan shark hesitated, and the old man grew red in the face.

"Very well, sir," said Dale, "Look at my scars. I will march to jail down Main Street, and all Mobile shall witness the treatment of an old soldier."

His words spread through the town. In half an hour, a dozen of the most prominent people in Mobile lined up to pay the debt, and a full discharge was handed the old general.

Dale, while living in Monroe County, was elected to the Alabama Legislature in 1819 and several succeeding terms.

He was one of a committee who escorted General Lafayette to the capital of Alabama (Cahaba) in 1824. Dale moved to Perry County in 1830, and then bought land in Mississippi, and went to the Mississippi Legislature in 1836.

The old general — hero of the legendary canoe fight on the Alabama River — died May 23, 1841, at Daleville, Miss.

Chapter Seventeen

1814 A. D.

Horseshoe Bend: Fortress or death trap? Old Hickory wins his biggest battle in Alabama

About 10:30 on the morning of March 27, 1814, the first American troops pushed through the trees across the clearing from the jagged line of log breastworks.

A crag-faced man on a white horse came out of the woods, as the soldiers leaned on their rifles, resting after their four-hour march.

Andrew Jackson looked at the breastworks, logs stacked on each other, stretching across the hill, and he shook his head.

The Creeks had built themselves an almost-impregnable haven — protected on three sides by the Tallapoosa River, 120 yards wide, and on the fourth side, the cork stopper in the bottle — the line of breastworks.

A haven — or a death trap.

The Indians called the loop in the river Cholocco Itabixee, Horse's Flat Foot. Now, with the logs stacked across, they called it Tohopeka, the Fort. The Americans called it Horseshoe Bend.

Behind the logs stood more than a thousand Indian warriors, the flower of the Creek nation, gathered from Indian towns all over East Alabama. And they were ready to fight, to the death if need be, to save their lands from the white man.

General Jackson — his men called him Old Hickory, the Creeks called him Old Mad Jackson — pointed to a small hill on the right, and his men wheeled two small cannon into position among the trees.

Soon the guns were booming shots into the barricade, but the small cannon balls bounced crazily off the logs. They could hear the Indians laughing and jeering on the other side.

Jackson had sent his cavalry general, John Coffee, off to the right with his mounted troops to cross the river downstream and cut off any possible retreat.

Some Cherokees, fighting with Coffee, acted without orders and swam the river at the bottom of the loop. They seized some of the Creek canoes pulled up on the bank.

Under covering fire, they ferried more Cherokees

and American troops across the river, into the vulnerable lower end of the loop. They overpowered the few Indian rear guards, burned the Indian village, and advanced into the soft rear of the line of Indian warriors, stretched across the breastworks.

Jackson saw the smoke of the burning Indian village, and guessed what was happening. His troops behind the Indian line held the whip hand for the moment. But if Jackson hesitated on the front, they would be destroyed, since the Indians inside the loop far outnumbered them.

It was just past noon, about 12:30 p.m. when Jackson made his move. He held up his hand, and the drummers began the long slow deadly roll of attack.

Jackson's men — East Tennessee volunteers on the right, the tough regulars of the U.S. Army's 39th Regiment in the center, and the West Tennessee militia on the left — began to move out of the trees and across the clearing, toward the breastworks.

They began to run now, bayonets at the ready, as heavy rifle fire crackled through the logs. Through the gunfire, the long slow roll of the drummers continued.

Jackson knew the significance of that long drum roll. And his opponent on the other side of the logs heard the roll too, and he knew what it meant.

Jackson's opponent was a big-nosed square-faced Indian named Menawa, called Great Warrior by his braves. As a youth, he had been called Hothlepoya, the Crazy War Hunter, because of his daring exploits on the Tennessee frontier.

The great Shawnee chief, Tecumseh, had come to Alabama in 1811, making speeches to tribe after tribe. His message: All Indians should join together now and fight the white man to the death, before it is too late. If you don't fight, the white man will take your lands and you will be destroyed. He was right.

Menawa listened to Tecumseh, and his message made sense. Menawa joined the warlike Indians, the

Red Sticks, and became one of the principal war chiefs.

In voting for war or peace, Creeks tossed a stick into a pile at the meeting hall — red sticks for war, white sticks for peace. After Tecumseh's impassioned speech, the red sticks outnumbered the whites.

Jackson, now a successful planter and politician in Nashville, had led troops down into Alabama before, trying to quell the Indian rebellion.

On his last foray, most of his men left camp and went home when their enlistments ran out, and Jackson complained bitterly of their "mutiny."

But when the fire broke out on the Alabama frontier — the massacre of more than 500 people at Fort Mims — Gov. William Blount of Tennessee answered the pleas for help from the Alabamians.

He gathered another volunteer army, and Jackson's military muscle was strengthened by a regiment of U.S. Army regulars, diverted to Jackson's command.

On the morning before the march to Horseshoe Bend, Jackson remembered the lack of enthusiasm of the troops his last time down from Tennessee, and he issued an order:

"Any officer or soldier who flies before the enemy without being compelled to do so by superior force ... shall suffer death."

Inside the breastworks, Menawa had to contend with the Creeks' principal chief, a medicine man or prophet named Monahee, or Monahell.

The prophet got up early on the morning of March 27, and dressed in full chief's regalia. His body quivered as a thousand warriors watched, and gourds filled with stones rattled in the dawn as he entered a hypnotic trance.

When the Cherokees broke across the river in the rear of the Creek line, one historian says Monahell ordered the warriors to abandon their breastworks on the front and attack to their rear.

At this point, the story goes, Menawa killed Monahell, and ordered the braves to hold their positions on the breastworks.

As the Americans charged the logs, both Jackson and Menawa knew the battle was crucial.

If the Indians won the battle, it would encourage other Indians tribes to join in a confederation to hold the line against the white man, and a major war would come.

If the Americans won, they both knew the Indians' power would be broken, that the Americans would take the rich land of the American Southeast without any real trouble.

Now, the Americans reached the breastworks. Some of them lay in the clearing, wounded by Indian rifle balls and arrows. One of the wounded was Ensign Sam Houston, a young army officer later to become president of Texas.

The battle raged up and down the logs, bloody hand-to-hand combat, until about 3:30 p.m. Then the Americans and the bayonets swept the field, flowing across the logs, leaving more than 500 Indians dead.

The great chief, Menawa, fought like a madman. Wounded seven times, he lay beneath a pile of Indian bodies. He later crept to the river, hid beneath the water and breathed through a reed, and escaped in a canoe.

At nightfall, the sporadic fighting stopped, and Jackson stood a victor on the battlefield. The Battle of Horseshoe Bend catapulted him to national fame, and he was commissioned a major general in the regular U.S. Army.

A few months later, he led the Americans to victory over the British at the Battle of New Orleans, and this battle made him a national hero.

Fourteen years later, the military hero became President of the U.S., and walked into the White House, the first President from the frontier.

So, Horseshoe Bend — near the present city of Dadeville — was the first in a series of events: It pushed Jackson into prominence as an Indian fighter, and gave him a chance for glory at New Orleans, which opened the doors of the White House to him.

For the Creeks, it was the end as a people and a nation in the Southeast. Twenty years later, they left Alabama in rags, walking the "Trail of Tears" to the alien prairies of Oklahoma.

"The great chief, Menawa, fought like a madman. Wounded seven times, he lay beneath a pile of Indian bodies. He later crept to the river, hid beneath the water and breathed through a reed, and escaped in a canoe."

Chapter Eighteen

1814 A. D.

Courage in defeat: Red Eagle rides into Jackson's camp

The man in the white buckskins rode the big gray horse easily, confidently, up to the gate of the American stockade. The red feather plumed backward over his head, and the carcass of a deer hung over his saddle.

As he swung the horse through the log gate, some of the civilians looked at him — and looked again.

"Good God ... it's Red Eagle."

"Looky thar ... it's Bill Weatherford his own self."

Inside the log walls of the stockade, the rider looked up at a roughly-built gallows, rope hanging, knot ready. He knew it had been built for him.

More civilians came running now, women and children too, to look at him. Hate was in their eyes.

He leaned down, and in a quiet, cultured voice, asked an officer:

"Can you tell me where I might find General Jackson, sir?"

The officer gulped, and pointed toward Jackson's tent. Nearby soldiers cocked their muskets, aiming at the rider. He grinned at them, waiting.

A thin red-haired stick of a man came running out of the tent and stopped, stunned, when he saw the rider.

He looked back at the muskets, leveled at him, then back at the red-haired man.

"General Jackson, I am not afraid of you. I fear no man, for I am a Creek warrior. I have nothing to request in behalf of myself; you can kill me, if you desire. But I come to beg you to send for the women and children of the war party who are now starving in the woods.

"Their fields and cribs have been destroyed by your people, who have driven them to the woods without an ear of corn. I hope that you will send out parties, who will safely conduct them here, in order that they be fed."

The civilians crowded around his horse. A woman, survivor of Fort Mims, started a chant: "kill him ... kill him ... kill him."

The red-haired man held up his hand.

The rider looked at the civilians around him, and saw the hatred flowing from their eyes, and he looked at Jackson again.

"I exerted myself in vain to prevent the massacre of the women and children at Fort Mims. I am now done fighting. The Red Sticks are nearly all killed. If I could fight you any longer, I would most heartily do so. Send for the women and children. They never did you any harm. But kill me, if the white people want it done."

The woman, her fists clenched, began the chant again: "kill him ... kill him ..."

Jackson held up his hand for silence, but the chant went on.

"*Silence*," he bellowed, and the noise subsided.

"Any man who would kill as brave a man as this would rob the dead."

Jackson invited Weatherford to dismount, Weatherford gave him the deer as a present, and they went into Jackson's tent.

They drank a glass of brandy, and Weatherford again gave Jackson his word he would fight no more. Jackson, impressed with Weatherford's audacity and bravery, let him go.

For Weatherford, called "Red Eagle" by the Creeks, that April day in 1814 was the low point in his life.

He was the son of a Scot trader named Charles Weatherford and an Indian princess, one of the ruling Wind Clan of the Creeks.

Alexander McGillivray, the Emperor of the Creeks, was his uncle.

Weatherford grew up in a time of troubles for the Creeks. Between 1800 and 1812, a wave of white settlers surged into Alabama from Georgia, South Carolina and Tennessee.

The Indians — Creeks in East and Central Alabama, Chickasaws in the north and west, Cherokees in the north, Choctaws in the southwest — were worried that the white people would gobble up their lands.

A great Shawnee chief named Tecumseh came south from Michigan, urging all the Indian tribes to fight together to save their lands.

A Choctaw chief named Pushmataha argued against Tecumseh's holy war. The white men had helped the Indians to learn farming, had helped their children to learn to read and write. Many of the Choctaws, Chickasaws and Cherokees joined the white men in the war against the Creeks.

The lines were drawn. The Creeks would fight to keep their lands, and the white men would vanquish the Creeks to open Alabama to the whites.

The fighting began at the Battle of Burnt Corn in Conecuh County. Then, in August of 1813, Weatherford — now the war chief of the Creeks — led a thousand Indian warriors against Fort Mims. The fort was just west of the present town of Tensaw, on the Alabama River, above Mobile.

Of the 553 people inside the stockade at Fort Mims, the Indians slaughtered more than 500. One report says Weatherford was sickened by the massacre, and rode away while it was going on.

The Fort Mims massacre set off tremors of fear along the Alabama frontier. The white people were afraid for their lives, they saw Indians behind every bush.

Gen. F. J. Claiborne moved against the Creeks, who were gathered at the Holy Ground, a high bluff on the Alabama River near Powell's Ferry in Lowndes County.

The Creeks prophets told the warriors that the white man's bullets would not hurt them, as long as they stood on the Holy Ground.

Not so. Claiborne and his men attacked, and the bullets brought Indian blood.

The Indians fled, and Weatherford found himself, alone, on a 15-foot bluff overlooking the river. He looked behind him, and the white soldiers were coming. He backed his gray horse, patted him on the rump, and spurred him forward.

The horse leaped off the bluff, Weatherford astride him, and they splashed beneath the water. Horse and rider surfaced, Weatherford holding the horse's mane with one hand, his rifle with the other.

The horse swam to the far shore, escaping the splashes of the bullets on both side.

The soldiers on the bluff knelt to fire at him, but the shots plunked harmlessly into the water. Weatherford turned as he reached the far shore, held his rifle high, and shouted a war cry to the soldiers.

Finally, Gov. William Blount of Tennessee sent a volunteer army down to subdue the Creeks. The army was led by the spindly red-haired general named Andrew Jackson, a planter and businessman out of Nashville.

Jackson had his troubles. On his first trip, he fought the Creeks twice, results inconclusive. Then Jackson's soldiers began drifting back to Tennessee, as their enlistments ran out.

A frustrated Jackson built another army, this time with a nucleus of regulars, and penned the Indians in the decisive battle of Horseshoe Bend on the Tallapoosa.

Some say Weatherford fought at Horseshoe Bend, and escaped.

Others say he recognized the bend in the Tallapoosa as a death trap, and refused to allow his contingent of warriors to go there.

And death trap it was. Jackson sprang it. His soldiers stormed the Creek breastworks and killed almost all of the Creek warriors inside.

The battle sounded the death knell for the Creek nation. Jackson, in his ruthless treaty, took away most of the Creek heartland across the middle of Alabama (and also most of the Choctaw, Chickasaw and Cherokee lands from his amazed allies).

The remaining part of the Creek nation was ceded to the white men in 1832, and the remaining Creeks walked across the "Trail of Tears" to exile in Oklahoma.

After Horseshoe Bend, Weatherford saw that further fighting was useless, and rode into Fort Jackson, where Jackson had taken his army after Horseshoe Bend.

When Jackson let him go, Weatherford found a

tough life. Kinfolk of people scalped at Fort Mims blamed him, and stalked him, trying to kill him.

Finally, the pressure against him lessened, and Weatherford became a respected citizen in the lower part of Monroe County. Here, he had a plantation, a number of slaves, and a comparatively pleasant life.

In 1826, he joined his neighbors on a bear hunt, over-exerted himself, and died of fatigue.

Was he a villain? A heartless murderer? Or was he a brave man, an Indian King Canute, who tried his best to stem the white tide and keep Indian lands for the Indians? The answer lies with you.

Epilogue

Who was right, Menawa or Andrew Jackson?

Andrew Jackson prevailed, of course, because the primitive Indian society could not stand up against the weaponry and the aggressiveness of the Industrial Revolution.

But where does right lie? What would we have done, if we had been there? Would we have left the Indians in place, left them to continue in their woodland ways, growing a few crops and hunting for food? Probably not.

Menawa, if he stepped back among us today, might say: You told me the Indians would not have to go to the West. You signed treaties, saying they would not have to go. Yet you forced us out, you pushed us out of our homeland, you broke your treaties with us.

Furthermore, I helped you, and you promised that I would not have to go. Yet you forced me out, your broke your word with me. What kind of people are you?

And Andrew Jackson, if he could come back among us for a moment, might say: Look around you. Look at your house, your car, your cities, your way of life. Do you like these things? Would you rather that the

Indians had the land?

Would you rather see Indian villages instead of your cities, unbroken woods instead of highways and farms? Do not be so quick to blame us, for what we did 140 years ago. Consider that what we did, we did for ourselves. But we also did it for you.

There is no answer, of course. Both were right, in their ways. But the pure, hard pressure of an advancing civilization made things happen.

There was no way to keep white people from advancing across the continent of North America. There was no way to stop the cities and the farms. If you start with the pressure of population, pushing into America from Europe, we can see that whatever Menawa did, whatever Andrew Jackson did, the same thing would have happened.

So that's where Alabama stood, around 1815. Jackson had beaten the Creeks at Horseshoe Bend, and the Indian power was broken in the Southeast. White settlers pushed west from Georgia into the Mississippi Territory, and more settlers poured through the Cumberland Gap into Kentucky and Tennessee, and ranged downward into the state which was to become Alabama.

As 1820 approached, the settlements grew — at Huntsville on the Tennessee River, at Tuscaloosa on the Warrior, at Selma and Montgomery on the Alabama River, and at Mobile on the coast.

It was the Mississippi Territory, stretching from the Georgia line to the Mississippi River, and the settlers on the Alabama river system — the Tennessee, the Black Warrior and the Alabama — were bound together by the rivers. They traveled the rivers — the steamboat was coming into its own, and they traded with each other.

They formed bonds, of trade and family and communication, and they let Washington know: We want to be a state by ourselves, we don't want to be governed by a faraway government on the Mississippi River.

So, as 1819 approached, the pressure built. The Alabama settlers wanted a state of their own, tied together by their life-giving rivers.

In 1819, they got their wish: A new state. Alabama. Named after the Alibamo Indian tribe. Some say it means, in Indian language, "Here we rest."

In my next book, you will watch a young state grow. I will tell you the stories of the raw new place — the growing pains, the political fights between the people who lived on different rivers, the heroes, the heroines, the villains, and the stories of the great steamboats, skimming along the Alabama rivers.

In it, I will tell you the stories, I will show you the people, of a new state called Alabama.

About the author

Clarke Stallworth grew up in Thomaston, a small town of 300 people in the Black Belt cotton region of South Alabama.

In his early teen years, Stallworth had two paper routes, one in the morning and one in the evening, so he became familiar with newspapers and the printed word early in life.

He tells of his "space ship," a green front porch swing at his home. He discovered books along with newspapers, and spent all his newspaper profits on books. With no library in town, he ordered a steady stream of books from mail-order publishers.

And in that front porch swing, as hundreds of

loaded cotton wagons lined up to gin (the tiny town had three gins), he escaped the small town. With books, he could swim the Hellespont with Richard Halliburton, work alongside a coolie in a rice field with Pearl Buck, fight the Fascists in Spain with Ernest Hemingway.

He served as a seaman in the Navy during World War II, was called back in the Korean War and served as a lieutenant on a destroyer off Korea. He attended journalism school at the University of North Carolina, and came to Birmingham as a cub reporter on *The Birmingham Post* in 1948, covering the Ku Klux violence in 1949. At one point, a Klansman threw a hammer at his head, but missed.

As a reporter for *The Birmingham Post-Herald*, he covered the Phenix City cleanup by the Alabama National Guard and the Phenix City murder trials in 1954 and 1955. For his work in Phenix City, he was nominated for the Pulitzer Prize and won the Associated Press Sweepstakes for the best newspaper story in Alabama in 1954.

Beginning in 1956, he covered the Folsom, Patterson and Wallace administrations in the state capitol, and won AP newswriting prizes for eight straight years. He became city editor of *The Birmingham Post-Herald* in 1963, and directed the coverage of Birmingham's racial troubles. He served as managing editor of The *Columbus* (Ga.) *Ledger-Enquirer* in 1965 and 1966, returning to Birmingham to become city editor of *The Birmingham News*.

As city editor and managing editor of *The News*, he continued to write. He covered the opening day of the Vietnam talks in Paris in 1969, and wrote about the crushing defeat of freedom in Prague, as Russian tanks circled the city.

In 1979, he visited Cuba and wrote a series about life under the special brand of Cuban communism.

In 1980, he began a column called "Alabama Journey," wandering around the state, talking to interesting people. And he began a Sunday column of stories out of Alabama history, called "A Day in the Life of Alabama."

Stallworth retired from *The Birmingham News* in 1991, after 42 years in the newspaper business. He is now a writing consultant, doing workshops for newspaper reporters and editors. He has done more than 100 workshops for press associations in 40 states across the U.S. and Canada.

He has conducted 33 workshops for The American Press Institute in Reston, Va., and has taught journalism at the University of Alabama, Samford University, and the University of Alabama at Birmingham.

Stallworth is married to novelist Anne Nall Stallworth. Their daughter, Carole Stallworth Bennighof, is a music teacher in Birmingham, and their son, Clarke Stallworth III, is an art teacher at Ohio State University.